from Psychosomatics to Soma-Semiotics

from

PSYCHOSOMATICS

to

SOMA-SEMIOTICS

Felt Sense and the Sensed Body

in Medicine and Psychotherapy

Peter Wilberg

ISBN 978-1-904519-11-9

CONTENTS

Preface   7

Introduction
...science, sense and semiotics   21

Towards a Semiotics of Felt Sense
...making sense of signs   42

The Semiotics of Felt Sense in Psychotherapy
... from signified sense to sensed significance   56

The Semiotics of Felt Sense in Somatic Medicine
...from psychosomatics to soma-semiotics   72

Sensing the Patient's Felt Dis-ease
...from medical diagnosis to organismic resonance   95

Summary
...somatic resonance in medicine and mental health   159

Appendix
....subjective biology and biosemiotics   177

Bibliography   206

Preface

This collection of selected essays draws upon my own experience as a therapist in order to introduce and weave together a number of different frameworks and perspectives I have found to be most helpful and enlightening. My aim is to show their mutual significance to one another and to a new 'soma-semiotic' understanding of (a) semiotics as such - the study of signs and of their relation to meaning or 'sense' (b) the significance of this relation in the therapist-client relationship and (c) its relevance to understanding the nature of illness and to affirming the *medical* relevance of psychotherapy for clients suffering from serious or chronic somatic illness.

At the heart of this work is the fundamental thesis that illnesses have *meanings* rather than causes or cures, an understanding that still forms no part of orthodox biomedical training or practice – or even that of most forms of 'complementary' medicine. Semiotics, as the study of signs, can offer an alternative to all *causal* models of disease etiology, by recognising the *sign* character of somatic symptoms, and their role in giving expression to – signifying - the patient's subjectively felt dis-ease. In contrast to the 'physical' body', the body as perceived from without, the individual's subjective or *felt* body is not, in principle the object of any possible form of external biomedical examination, testing or treatment.

The term 'soma-semiotics' is used in contrast to both psychosomatic, bio-psycho-social or 'psychogenic' approaches to somatic illness - all of which to some degree merely offer alternative *causal* models of disease etiology. It is also used in distinction to the term 'biosemiotics', which today constitutes a very mixed array of theoretical perspectives - ranging from those which merely use semiotic metaphors such as 'marker', 'signalling' 'message' or 'recognition' to support a form of molecular reductionism (reducing the 'language of life' to its genetic-molecular alphabet and vocabulary) to others which regard the 'sign' rather than the molecule as the basic 'unit' of life, but which rely on old models of the relation of signs to meaning or sense.

The most fundamental difference between biosemiotics and soma-semiotics – and the principle contribution that the latter offers to semiotics as such – lies in the fundamental distinction it draws between what I term the *signified sense* of any given phenomenon on the one hand (for example the already signified medical sense or meaning of a patient's bodily or behavioural symptoms) and its immediately felt meaning or *sensed significance*.

This distinction draws upon Eugene Gendlin's concept of 'bodily sensing', 'felt sense' or 'felt bodily sense' and the therapeutic practice of 'Focusing' through which it is applied. The key to Focusing is a practice of 'resonating back and forth' between one's *wordless bodily sense* of a given situation or feeling of dis-ease and its formulated and formed expression in mental words and images. Only in this way can one come to the fitting or 'full' word. Language or 'signifiers' in full resonance with felt sense bring about what Gendlin calls a 'felt shift' in one's state of being - rather than foreclosing felt sense by signifying it with habitual, ready-to-hand words and concepts. The premature *foreclosure* of felt sense is perhaps the most serious vocational danger, if not disease, of the therapist or physician indoctrinated through their training with a specific theoretical language or sign system - one which then becomes their principal means of 'semiosis', the process of 'making sense' of a person's behavioural, verbal or bodily signs.

Soma-semiotics recognises also an intimate relation between the innately therapeutic practice of Focusing and Rupert Sheldrake's theoretical concept of 'morphic resonance'. It reinterprets the essence of *morphic resonance* precisely as a relation of *resonance* (or dissonance) between felt sense or 'sensed significance' on the one hand, and its expression in any type of *signified sense* or signifying *form* (Greek *morphe*). Signified sense is understood as *giving form* to sensed significance, whether in the form of significant phenomena or events, of words or mental images, or of signifying somatic 'signs' - symptoms.

The roots of both biosemiotics and 'soma-semiotics' can be traced back to the work of biologist Jakob von Uexküll (1864-1944), for it was Uexküll who laid the basis of what I term 'subjective biology'. He did so through the radical insight that each form of organism dwells in its own unique subjective world or 'environment', a world shaped by its own *highly selective* and *species-specific* modes of perception and response to particular sensory signs or 'cues', signs whose significance is immediately sensed and enacted. As human beings, there is no way we can experience the sonar world of a bat, the visual world of a fly, or the olfactory world of a dog.

Like other species of organisms, as human beings we too dwell in our own unique subjectively perceived 'life world', a world of meaning that addresses us and that calls upon us to respond in ways that constitute meaningful, signifying acts in the life world of others.

A 'life world' is a world of both signs and senses, of both, uniquely felt or *sensed significances* on the one hand and of conventionally or consensually *signified senses* on the other.

It was the 'subjective biology' of Uexküll (see Appendix) that may also have germinated Heidegger's understanding of human existing or *Da-sein* as something which cannot be objectified at all under any circumstances for its essence is *"a capacity to receive-perceive the significance of the things that are given to it and that address it...".*

It was Heidegger who also introduced three profound insights central to soma-semiotics:

1. That the body is no 'thing' but an activity – the activity of bodying.

   "We know by now a great deal – almost more than we can encompass – about what we call the body, without having seriously thought about what bodying is. It is something more and different from merely 'carrying a body around with one'."

*"Every feeling is an embodiment attuned in this or that way, **a** mood that embodies in this or that way."*

2. That *"All explanation reaches only so far as the explication of that which is to be explained".*

3. Thus *"To be in a position to explain an illness genetically, we need first of all to explain what the illness in itself is. It can be that a true understanding of the essence of an illness...prohibits all causal-genetic explanation..."*

4. The distinction between the (subjectively) felt or lived body (German *Leib*) and the body as a mere objective physiological 'corpus' (German *Körper*).

Soma-semiotics also draws nourishment and inspiration from the words of the German Jewish thinker Martin Buber:

"Signs happen to us without respite; living means being addressed ...What happens to me addresses me ... Only by sterilizing it, by removing the seed of address from it, can I take what happens to me as a part of a world-happening which does not intend me. ... From out of this tower of the ages the objection will be levelled against me, if some of its doorkeepers should pay any attention to such trains of thought, that it is nothing but a variety of superstition to hold that cosmic and telluric happenings have for

the life of the human being a direct meaning that can be grasped. For instead of understanding an event physically, biologically, sociologically ... these keepers say that an attempt is being made to get behind the event's alleged significance, and for this there is no place in a reasonable world continuum of space and time. Thus then, unexpectedly, I seem to have fallen into the company of augurs of whom, as is well known, there are remarkable modern varieties. But whether they haruscape or cast a horoscope their signs have this peculiarity – that they are in a dictionary, even if not necessarily a written one. It does not matter how esoteric the information that is handed down: he who searches the signs is 'well up' in what ... this or that sign means. Nor does it matter that special difficulties of separation and conjunction are created by the meeting of signs of different types. For you can 'look it up in the dictionary'."

Yet *"What happens to me says something to me. But what it says cannot be revealed by any esoteric information; for it has never been said before ... it can neither be interpreted or translated; I can have it neither explained nor displayed; it is not a 'what' at all, it is said into my very life ..."*

Unfortunately, the type of 'dictionary' Buber refers to has evermore modern varieties, both esoteric *and* exoteric – not least the vocabularies of different approaches to 'therapy' and 'counselling', the diagnostic manuals of medicine and psychiatry, the textbooks of the sciences - or the bodies of dry theoretical constructs on which different specialised academic disciplines feed on and seek to jealously guard from one another.

What I term 'soma-semiotics has no such academic guardians or gatekeepers and is not another new gated 'discipline'. Instead it is the *signifier* of a new *trans-disciplinary* approach to all that was previously herded into the safekeeping of a discipline called psychosomatics' – a discipline still misunderstood as dealing with a borderline or marginal set of conditions which could not be clearly identified as either purely 'psychological' or purely 'somatic', or that embraces 'psycho-social' as well as purely biological factors in understanding the etiology of somatic illness.

And yet the very separation of 'mental' and 'physical' illness, 'mind' and 'body', 'psyche' and 'soma' is challenged by the central message of soma-semiotics. This is that healing illness of any nature (including so-called 'mental' illness) is essentially a matter of 'coming to our senses' in the most literal sense of this phrase – restoring and invigorating our immediate sensory experience, both of our own bodies and of the world around us, yet doing so without in any way seeking to signify - to label or diagnose – what it is that we are aware of sensing. Only by giving ourselves time to fully *feel and follow* any symptom or sense of dis-ease can we also come to directly sense its significance – not by interpreting it as a sign in any way but by letting it *become* a sign, one which points us to the specific life problem or dilemma of which it is an expression. Only by staying with and following our 'felt sense' of dis-ease in this way will it also *transform* of its own accord, having done its job of calling upon us to be aware of it and to feel it – thus leading us to a sense of what it is in our lives that it is there to point us to. Any symptom, felt and followed in a purely sensual way, through felt sense and our felt body, will reveal its meaning or sense and in doing so become redundant as a sign. This is the healing meaning and benefit of 'soma-semiotics' in contrast to both orthodox biomedical diagnoses, psychosomatic explanations or the alternative 'causes' and 'cures' offered by complementary medicine – itself no real 'alternative' to the simple process of making sense of illness directly – through coming back to and staying with our senses, our immediate 'felt sense' of our body, self and world.

What comes in the way of 'coming to our senses' – of once again recognising innate meaning or sense in immediate sensory experiencing – is the prejudice that sense-perception is always and already a perceiving 'as'. Thus the fact that as human beings we perceive a table *as* a table – and that totally irrespective of its exact sensory form and qualities - would seem to indicate that sense perception itself has a *sign* character – the very tableness of the table being a mere *sign* of something we can sit around or eat on - and this sign character of the table being also its essential meaning or *sense*. And yet this a purely human prejudice, modelled principally on the sense of sight.

Merely seeing a table *as* a table - or a painting as the *representation* of a table - *that* is truly the most 'abstract' mode of perception and appreciation of meaning - one that reduces meaning to an already signified sense of what we perceive – thus *desensualising* sense perception itself and reducing to a mere recognition of signs.

The desensualisation of sensory experiencing is a cultural plague of our era. For whether in watching TV ads or passing through a shopping mall, we are assaulted by a barrage of sensory images or objects all of which are dominated by their sign character – as branded commodities asking to be noticed and bought. Even the beach sunset displayed on the TV ad is nothing to be truly seen or sensed, but a mere conventionalised *sign* for promoting commercial travel packages and destinations.

If, in contrast, we take hearing music rather than seeing tables as our paradigm, there is no way in which our direct sensual appreciation of the meaning of music is dependent on hearing its phrases, chords, melodies, tone colours and patterns 'as' some nameable or usable thing. Music is a key to *not* sensing *as* – but instead finding meaning or sense directly in sensory experiencing itself. The same applies to those so-called 'abstract' visual arts which confound our attempts to reduce the configuration of shape and colours we behold to some nameable thing - but rather open our eyes to the innately sensuous meaning of those sensory shape and colours.

It was through interweaving the Focusing methods of Gendlin, the 'subjective biology' of Jakob von Uexküll, Sheldrake's concept of 'morphic fields', and insights from the Seth books of Jane Roberts, that I came to an understanding of all organisms, not least the human organism, as essentially composed of organising *field patterns* of subjectivity or awareness itself - each of which in turn shapes its own patterned field of awareness or 'environment'. Organising field patterns of awareness constitute the very *syntax* of life from a soma-semiotic perspective. Yet they are comparable less to verbal syntax and linguistic patterns than to musical patterns of tone – for they are essentially patterned *tonalities* of awareness. These can be *sensed* as silent, pre-linguistic tones of *feeling* or 'feeling tones' - as described by Seth in the passage below:

"Your emotional feelings are often transitory, but beneath there are certain qualities of feeling uniquely your own, that are like deep musical chords. While your day-to-day feelings may rise or fall, these characteristic feeling tones lie beneath. Sometimes they rise to the surface, but in great long rhythms. You cannot call these negative or positive. They are instead tones of your being. These feeling tones then, pervade your being ... From them, from your core, your flesh arises.

Everything that you experience has consciousness, and each consciousness is endowed with its own feeling-tone. Your flesh springs about you in response to these inner chords of your being, and the trees, rocks, seas and mountains spring up as the body of the earth from the deep inner chords within the atoms and molecules, which are also living."

Seth, in *The Nature of Personal Reality* by Jane Roberts

Like vocal or musical tones, feeling tones can possess and combine any number of *sensual qualities* such as brightness and darkness, lightness and heaviness, flatness and sharpness, clarity and dullness, as well as diverse tone colours, textures and 'shapes'. It is these sensual qualities of feeling tone that find expression in all the sensory phenomena experienced in both our dream and waking world, as well as in qualities and patterns of muscle and nerve tone, cell and organ tone, including vocal tone. The organism then, is truly a proto-musical 'instrument' or *organon* - one whose two principle 'functions' are (a) *dreaming* and (b) *bodying* specific tonal patterns and sensual qualities of awareness.

'Soma-semiotics' is in this sense no more radical in principle than the recognition that, just as the richly *sensual* patterns and qualities of instrumental tones that constitute *music* do not 'signify' or 'represent' meanings but instead possess innate meaning or *sense* – so too do *all sensory qualities and phenomena* – including the *sensations and symptoms* of dis-ease and illness in all its forms.

In acknowledging the fundamentally subjective character of the human organism and describing its primordial functions as *bodying* and *dreaming*, I acknowledge also Arnold Mindell's notion of the 'dreambody' or 'dreaming body', which he used to designate what Heidegger called the lived body (*Leib*) and which I term - following Gendlin's use of term 'felt sense' - the 'felt body'. Mindell's daring lay in encouraging patients to choose to 'amplify' their suffering – to *sense* their pain or other symptoms *more* intensely rather than less. What he found was that through this process of amplification an individual's *dis-ease* would sooner or later transform and dissolve of its own accord –

releasing dream-like insights into its own felt meaning or *sense* - and thus no longer needing to take form as bodily symptoms or *signs* of disease.

It is not within the scope of this book to explore the soma-semiotics of *dreaming* as such. Instead it suffices to say that from a soma-semiotic perspective, somatic symptoms can indeed be compared to dream symbols, and illnesses to *embodied* dreams or nightmare – to 'body dreams' given form through the 'dreaming body'.

From this perspective it makes no more sense to deny *meaning* to bodily symptoms than it does to deny meaning to dream symbols, just as it makes no more sense to diagnose or 'cure' an illness through medication than it does to medically 'cure' a dream or nightmare. In this context, due respect must also be given to Freud's implicitly semiotic analysis of the hidden 'word' of the dream, as well as to what, in his very last years, he came to see as the *second fundamental principle* of psychoanalysis – one that has been largely ignored and yet deconstructs the dualism still implicit in the term 'psychosomatics'. For according to this principle of Freud, what is most *quintessentially* 'psychical' reveals itself *primarily* in what were previously thought of only as parallel, consequent or concomitant *somatic* phenomena.

Introduction

...science, sense and semiotics

The starting point of science or any mode of knowledge seeking is, as Martin Heidegger emphasised, not the supposed 'evidence' of that science but the adoption by a human being – the scientist – of a specific stance or standpoint, attitude or bearing towards the world. The defining theoretical stance of modern science is one of treating the world as something which stands over and against an independent 'subject' or 'observer', and consists of a set of 'objects'. These objects however are already posited or 'pre-sup-posed' in advance by theoretical concepts of them – concepts which science essentially treats as more essentially real than the tangible, *subjectively* experienced phenomena they are used to 'explain'.

What we take as 'science' today effectively takes its objects as 'given' through a type of tacit, unquestioning consensus based on what Heidegger called "the theoretical comportment". This is a comportment which abstracts from all *pre-theoretical* dimensions of human sensual experiencing – and of meaning or 'sense' itself. Thus 'causes' and 'cures' are sought by 'medical science' for some objective and potentially life threatening 'thing' called 'illness' or 'disease' – yet without even beginning to question what illness as such essentially *is*, without seeking to make sense of its *meaning* for the individual, and without even recognising the fundamental difference between diagnosed diseases and the individual's immediately felt, bodily sense of 'dis-ease'.

The human body itself is treated by biomedical science as a mere *object* of 'evidence-based' research rather than as an embodiment of the *human being* – its living biological language. In other words the human being *as such* – not being anything measurable – does not even figure in the entire literature and language of medical, biological and genetic *accounts* of the human body - save as a statistical non-entity.

Heidegger saw the basic stance of modern 'scientific method' as one essentially irreconcilable with the fundamental aims of science *as* science – that of search for and discernment (*scire*) of truth. In place of an understanding of truth based on the standpoint of a *disembodied* scientific observer or 'subject' standing over and against a world of consensually agreed objects, Heidegger insisted that true 'understanding' meant recognising one's own being as *embedded* from the start in an already *embodied* and meaningful relation *to* the world – and therefore not capable, in principle, of separation from the world – the illusory stance of the scientific 'observer'. Authentic knowledge or 'science' meant grounding truth and meaning in an immediate, *bodily* and *pre-theoretical* awareness of the sense or meaning of phenomena.

Truly 'making sense' of things in this way requires that we first of all recognise the shared conceptual pre-suppositions and common sense assumptions that govern both our 'scientific' and everyday views of reality – in other words, the hidden 'semiotic' or 'sense-making' practices that shape this 'reality'. These semiotic practices take the form of tacitly agreed codes of discourse, conduct and communication that shape the way we make sense of phenomena. It is through these tacitly agreed modes of 'sense-making' that an agreed 'con-sensual' understanding of reality – what the phenomenological sociologist Alfred Schutz called a 'we world' – is socially and semiotically constructed and sustained.

Three basic semiotic codes can be broadly delineated:

1. *A code of discourse* in which we tacitly assume a shared understanding of the meaning or 'sense' of commonly used terms, words and utterances.

2. *A code of conduct* governing everyday worldly practices whereby their own commonly accepted sense or 'rationale' is also tacitly assumed.

3. *A code of communication* that sets boundaries on the legitimate doubt that can be cast on the commonly accepted senses of words and the commonly accepted sense or rationale of worldly practices.

Together, these codes constitute a set of tacit or unspoken agreements and rules which together establish what Harold Garfinkel called *points of departure* for any specific social action or interaction, practice or procedure. *Departing* from these rules or questioning these points of departure, is, as Harold Garfinkel's studies showed, guaranteed to arouse bewilderment or indignation.

As an example, we can identify three socially-accepted points of departure for a typical medical consultation:

It is tacitly understood that we all know what 'illness' and 'health' are, that they are opposites, and that 'illness' is something 'bad' and 'health' something 'good'.

It is tacitly understood that the patient arranges the consultation because he is suffering symptoms of a possible 'illness' which he wishes to have identified and which he is therefore prepared to be prescribed treatment for.

It is tacitly understood that the patient will describe their symptoms and that the medical practitioner will then seek to arrive at a medical diagnosis of an illness, and recommend a course of treatment aimed at a 'cure', and based on knowledge of the organic physical 'cause' of that illness.

Should a patient reject any or all of these points of departure, or depart from any of the unspoken rules of interaction they give rise to, he or she will be regarded as disruptive or deviant. This often happens in the case of psychiatric patients who may seek help from a medical practitioner but who may doubt that they are 'ill', doubt that they are in need of 'treatment' or doubt that they suffering from symptoms with an organic cause.

Scientific sense, in contrast to 'common sense', places, in principle, no boundaries on legitimate doubt or questionability. In practice however, the situation is quite different. For being itself a social practice, modern science is governed by its own codes of discourse, conduct and communication, and by the points of departure implied by these codes.

What Garfinkel called 'ethnomethodology' was not itself a 'methodology' but referred rather to the observation and study of the actual 'methods' or 'practices' by which - in their everyday interaction and communication, and in their everyday life and work – people both coded and made sense of these interactions and this communication – their 'semiotic' codes and practices. One of Garfinkel's own experimental techniques therefore, was to deliberately disrupt the conventional semiotic 'codes' of everyday interactions and interpersonal communication. He did this by daring his students participate in them in a wholly impersonal 'scientific' manner – as if ignorant of the required codes, and adopting an attitude to 'semiosis; or sense-making akin to Cartesian doubt or Socratic questioning.

Example:
Subject: Hi, Ray. How is your girlfriend feeling?
Experimenter: What do you mean "How is she feeling?" Do you mean physically or mentally?
Subject: I mean how is she feeling. What's the matter with you?

Garfinkel was struck by the bewilderment and intensity of the emotions aroused by disrupting routinised conversational exchanges based on tacit consensual understandings and semiotic codes. The example chosen may nevertheless appear facile - and certainly does not do justice to the sophistication and originality of Garfinkel's studies of interactions and communication in several specific institutional and vocational contexts. In contrast, an example of Eugene Gendlin's technique of 'focusing' is far from facile, even at first glance. For here, instead of seeking to disrupt common sense by challenging people to intellectually define the meaning of common consensually understood words or phrases, the focus is on their tangibly felt bodily sense of what it is that these words actually name.

Example:
Subject: I've been upset all day since the meeting.
Focuser: Bring your awareness into your chest and belly and just spend a minute silently focusing on how you feel this 'upsetness' in your body.
Subject: What do you mean? I feel upset.
Focuser: I'm asking you to sense how that upsetness feels in your chest and belly.

Subject: It's as if something sticky is turning around and around in my belly.

Focuser: Try recalling your body's felt sense of the whole thing, the whole meeting – to feel the connection between it and the sticky thing turning around.

Subject: That's it. The meeting began all right and I felt good but then there came a sticky point at which I knew I just I wouldn't be able to turn things around.

Focuser: OK, so focus now for a time on recalling your body's felt sense of what stopped that turnaround from happening.

Subject: As I began to feel frustrated I just got more and more in my head, feeling out of my body whilst trying to score intellectual points by squeaking at people in a high-pitched tone of voice.

Focuser: OK. So focus now on what it might have felt like to stay grounded in your body, to let yourself feel the sense of frustration in your chest and belly rather than letting it get to your head and come out in your voice.

Subject: Funny. As I did what you suggested the sticky thing stopped turning over in my belly and I felt something else, like a solid core that felt patient and unperturbed rather than upset.

Though the terms 'psychotherapy' and 'psychotherapist' have a consensually agreed meaning and though they refer to accepted social practices with their own points of departure and semiotic codes, Gendlin questioned the very idea that there is such a thing as 'psychotherapy' or 'psychotherapists'. He argued instead that there were only dialogues between people – any people – dialogues that could be more or less therapeutic. What makes a dialogue therapeutic in Gendlin's sense has nothing to do with knowledge of some 'thing' we call the *psyche*, or with psychotherapy as a social practice. A therapeutic dialogue is one that breaks a basic common sense code of discourse – the assumption that people share a common mental or emotional understanding of particular words or life situations, that these shared meanings constitute indubitable and unquestionable *psychical* realities, and that any exploration of our personally felt *somatic* sense of their meaning is therefore irrelevant.

As Gendlin points out, it is only on occasions when people lack words that they refer back to their proprioceptive, bodily sense of what they want to say. Similarly, it is only through *not* understanding or being understood by others that assumed and conventionalised understandings break down, and a breakthrough to a deeper, *felt* understanding becomes possible.

For as Garfinkel points out: "The anticipation that a person will be understood" is a "sanctioned property of common discourse".

What have a medical consultation or the nature of therapeutic dialogue to do with the defence of scientific methodology? Medicine and psychotherapy are areas where the modern scientific and everyday attitudes to sense-making meet. They are also areas in which an authentic scientific stance is *compromised* by a set of pre-established social scientific and social practices and sign systems which, being accepted *as a part* of everyday life, are neither socially nor scientifically questioned. The compromising of scientific methodology is particularly prevalent in professional practices such as medicine and psychotherapy.

A professional practitioner is someone who applies methods derived from an inherited body of scientific knowledge, and hopefully also keeps up to date with new research. A scientist is someone who not only learns how to apply certain methods more effectively but uses their own experience to add to and deepen the body of knowledge which was the source of those methods. Both the scientist and the professional practitioner begin by accepting an inherited body of knowledge on faith. But the professional practitioner, who is also a scientist – a knowledge seeker – goes on to question the limits and explore the gaps in this body of knowledge. There is no reason why an engineer, as a professional practitioner of an applied science, should of necessity also be a research scientist. But the same does not apply to a physician, psychiatrist or psychotherapist. A scientific physician or psychologist is someone motivated and able to learn something more about the human body and human beings from their every bodily encounter with another human being.

In the past, every physician was at the same time a scientist, gathering not only new experience but also gaining new scientific insights from that experience. The same was true of psychologists such as Freud. Today, however, we acknowledge entire professions of health 'practitioners' who do not feel any need to be scientists – who apply a general body of knowledge to particular individuals but have no interest in deriving new insights of *general* validity from their experience of particular patients or clients. Instead they see themselves only as professional practitioners – their sole job being to *incorporate* each new person's experiences into an existing or pre-given body of professional knowledge, to make sense of it in existing terms and respond to it according to their professional training. Such a 'know enough already' or 'know it all already' attitude may be 'scientifically' adequate for the job of a professional engineer, who is unlikely to discover new laws of mechanics building a bridge. It is wholly inadequate and inadmissible for a practitioner of the applied human sciences, who will invariably be confronted with scientifically significant *differences* in each new human being to whom the existing body of scientific knowledge is applied.

Thus the search for a standard and generic medical *diagnosis* replaces the development of new insights from *gnosis* – direct acquaintance with particular patients. The adoption of standard sense-making procedures applies no less in psychotherapy, alternative medicine and complementary health practices than in orthodox medicine and psychiatry. The practitioner seeks merely to identify and remedy a pre-classified 'condition' – whether an organic disorder or childhood disturbance, a chemical imbalance in a person's brain or an 'energy imbalance' in their 'aura', a blocked artery or blocked emotion or 'energy' or acupunctural 'meridians'.

Of chief concern to the 'professional' is the correct and effective application of a body of knowledge with which to make sense of and respond to the client's emotional signals or bodily symptoms. Of considerably lesser concern is the patient's or client's own semiotic process – the way they make sense of and respond to their felt condition and its felt sense or meaning. The client is expected only to *signify* their condition in conventionalised language that can be 'understood' and 'made sense of' by the professional, and to do so in a time-constrained context governed by its own already established semiotic codes, points of departure and routinised or ritualised procedures.

The current one-sided scientific definition of 'semiotics' as the study of signs rather than sense, together with the definition of 'semiosis' as the process of *sign making* rather than *sense-making* fits in well with the semiotic codes governing social and scientific practices in general, which are about 'making the right signs', using the 'right' discourse codes or jargons, and responding 'appropriately' to signs made by others – rather than *making deeper sense of those signs*. For this to happen professional practitioners must be able, according to Heidegger to "glance out beyond their profession and practice and...for once open themselves, let themselves into something entirely different."

The emergence of the modern scientific method shook the foundations and departed from the once universally shared assumptions of the pre-modern religious world view previously dominant in the West. Initially it was something "entirely different". However, the authentic scientific attitude has now been sacrificed to the semiotic codes governing its own institutionalised practice and to the scientific method as this is currently understood – a method largely applied in the service of corporate profit or to sustain the legitimacy of professional bodies. The continuing development of phenomenological science in defence of an authentic scientific stance and an authentically scientific methodology will in turn shake the foundations of the modern scientific method and revolutionise both the theoretical foundations and social practices stemming from that method. It will be grounded in the understanding of both human and natural phenomena as the expressions of fundamental semiotic processes – of *semiosis*.

This understanding was already implicit in the philosophy of Kant and found its first scientific expression in the biology of Jakob von Uexküll and in Freud's attempt to get to grip with the semiotic processes involved in dreaming and in the interpretation of dreams. It received a new and decisive direction from the fundamental ontology of Martin Heidegger, with its emphasis on the fundamental sense or meaning of Being or 'is-ness' as such. It takes its lead from both the 'ethnomethodology' of Harold Garfinkel and the 'focusing' methodology of Gendlin, implicit in both of which is a new *soma-semiotics* – a semiotics of immediately felt bodily or 'somatic' sensing of particular signs or 'signifiers'.

Not just linguistic signifiers but all phenomena have a semiotic or sign function. But signs do not exist in isolation. The sign function of a word has to do with its place within a larger pattern of linguistic *signification*. The sign function of a phenomenon has to with its place within a larger pattern of *significance*. A table is not just an extra-linguistic object to which we attach the verbal signifier 'table'. Even without naming it as such, the table already functions as a sign within a larger pattern of significance, being perceived as a place around which we can sit, a platform on which we can eat or write etc. The phenomenon is not merely 'a table' but, for example the table that someone bought at a bargain price just after getting married or moving house. Similarly, a street is no mere neutral object of perception. What I see of it or do not see of it is determined by its place within a larger pattern of significance. What I see is not 'a street' but *the* street I cross to get into my car or walk down to the local shop.

The semiotic dimension of phenomenology consists in understanding what a phenomenon *is* in terms of what it *means* to us – its place within a larger experiential context and larger patterns of significance, actual or potential.

What modern science, pre-modern religious world views and 'post-modernism' share in common however, is a search for a pre-given order or pattern of significance to events. Their common point of departure is the assumption of such a pre-given order, whether conceived of as divine, natural-scientific or 'semiotic' - in the narrow sense of having only to do with pre-established sign systems. Yet the essence of 'semiosis' is the process of emergence (*phusis*) of actually given patterns of significance from a field of *potential* patterns – in other words, the emergence of order from *pre-order*. 'Pre-order' however is not mere chaos or *disorder* but consists of potential patterns of significance or signification that are not themselves manifest as actual perceptual or linguistic phenomena. As such they cannot be perceived directly but only sensed. And yet it is all too easy to force our felt sense of new potential patterns of significance into the mould of actual and familiar ones.

Common, everyday sense-making and the consensual reality it assumes, consists of already established patterns of significance represented and reinforced by the accounts we give of them within already established languages or patterns of signification. Scientific sense too, seeks to fit new phenomena into already identified patterns of significance represented in the form of mathematical models or scientific 'laws'. Whether or not new experimental data fit these models is less important than the fact that in common with religion and common sense, science assumes a pre-given order of things that can ultimately be represented in one way or another. New models and the patterns of significance they represent, are created on the basis of earlier ones, and therefore however distinct from the latter, are at the same time inseparable from them and shaped by them. In social-scientific practices such as medicine, we see again the assumption of a pre-given order consisting of already established patterns of significance. Thus a patient's symptoms have meaning only as possible signs of a pre-given and already established disease pattern. Tests are conducted to either confirm or rule out the *actuality* of this possible disease pattern, without any regard to other *potential* patterns of significance unrecognised within the diagnostic framework of medical discourse.

The search for order in science, religion and common sense is self-fulfilling. For any pattern of significance, once identified, limits our awareness of alternate potential patterns and shapes our experience in a way that actively selects out phenomena that do not fit into established patterns or provide signs of other patterns. What Garfinkel called the 'documentary method' is a semiotic or 'sense-making' process whereby events are interpreted in terms of an already established pattern of significance, and thus provide further 'evidence' of the reality of that pattern. That the perceived pattern of significance itself may be represented in the form of *documents* (for example medical histories or case notes, business reports and legal reports, academic or scientific papers etc) is itself important – for these not only represent perceived commercial, legal, medical or scientific 'realities' according to their own semiotic codes and patterns of signification, but play a powerful role in the way these realities are perceived. Indeed, as documents they are *identified* with the very realities they document. Thus a set of medical test results or a scientific paper does not merely document a specific social practice – that of medical examination or scientific experimentation. As a document it also forms an important part of those practices, laying the basis for further tests or experiments.

The 'hypothesis' of a certain pattern of significance in phenomena can be confirmed by experiment or experience. Merely to confirm the phenomenal actuality of a particular pattern of significance however, by no means disproves the reality of *other* potential patterns, nor does it rule out the existence of alternate, actual patterns. The fact that a vast corpus of sentences, for example, can be shown to share the same syntactic pattern, does not disprove the reality of other potential patterns or the existence of sentences with different syntactic patterns. Similarly, the fact that a person or particle can be shown to exhibit a certain predictable pattern of behaviour proves neither that they do not also exhibit other patterns of behaviour, nor that they do not possess the potential for these other behaviours. In the modern scientific method, it is readily admitted that everything hinges on 'conditions' under which phenomena are observed to follow a predictable pattern, just as in daily life it is readily admitted that everything hinges on the 'situations' in which people behave in certain predictable ways. The question of how conditions or situations are defined, and to what degree they can be said to be 'the same' or 'different' is another matter however. Every determination of an experiential situation or set of experimental conditions is necessarily selective in what it counts as part of that situation or set of conditions.

The grounds of modern scientific and common sense rationality do not themselves fall within the scope of scientific experiment or everyday experience, both of which have their own pre-established rationale or *method* of sense-making. Within this rationale, the experiential conditions or experiential situations in which certain patterns of significance are observed are only 'controllable' or 'repeatable' in so far as they are pre-defined by the observer in a way that rules out conditions or aspects of a situation deemed to be irrelevant or not subject to direct observation, measurement or control. The idea that a population of human subjects, for example, can be *randomly* selected for a scientific experiment, is ultimately absurd. For any such selection, however unbiased in terms of definable criteria such as age, gender, racial background etc will be unbiased only according to those pre-defined criteria and not others. Indeed the very idea of a randomly 'indeterminate' sample of unique and highly determinate *individuals* is ultimately a contradiction in terms.

Conversely however, the different ways in which individuals can make sense of randomised events, and the number of patterns of significance they can find in them is limitless. This was shown by an experiment of Garfinkel's in which university students were asked to trial a new form of counselling in which they could ask the counsellor any series of questions and get a yes or no answer. Unknown to the subjects, the counsellor's yes-no answers were randomised and entirely arbitrary. This did not prevent the subjects from seeking and successfully finding deeply meaningful patterns of significance in the counsellor's answers – even where these appeared to directly contradict one another. Garfinkel's work demonstrated both the human being's unlimited capacity for sense-making and also the ways in which this capacity is limited by taken-for-granted significances attached to events and experiences in everyday life.

His studies however, ignored the role of *bodily sense* or meaning and the directly felt or sensed *body* in the human being's sense-making or semiotic activity.

In contrast, what Gendlin calls 'felt sense', i.e., *bodily sensing* and the *sensed body*, is central to what I term 'soma-semiotics' – this being an approach to mental and physical 'disease' based on a fundamental distinction between (a) the medically *signified sense* of any symptom or sign (its 'diagnostic' significance) and (b) the directly *sensed significance* of such signs for the patient, as the experience of a felt 'dis-ease'

Towards a Semiotics of Felt Sense

...making sense of signs

Eyes and ears are poor witnesses if we have souls that do not understand their language.
Heraclitus

Semiotics is the study of signs – and that means the study of life. For, we are surrounded by a world of signs. Everything we experience in our everyday world addresses us or 'speaks to us' in a certain way – it has a particular meaning or significance for us. In signifying particular meanings, all the events and phenomena we experience have a sign character. Our very perception of the world is a type of language, whose vocabulary consists of familiar and nameable things. What we perceive as everyday objects can be compared to 'words' in this perceptual vocabulary. Simply to see a tree as a tree, for example, requires that 'treeness' be a part of our visual vocabulary. The *sign function* of a phenomenon has to do with its place in a larger pattern of significance. We recognise a 'table' as a 'table' because we understand it as something we can sit around, eat on, use to place other objects on etc. But the *sensory* meaning of a phenomenon – its directly sensed significance - is something quite distinct from its place within such a larger pattern of significance or from seeing that phenomenon 'as' this or that. For the different dimensions of sensory experiencing are themselves languages – which is why it is that we can feel meaning in the colours of a sunset or piece of music even though neither represent or 'signify' anything. Instead their meaning or sense is felt as something immediately present in and as their sensory qualities of colour and tone.

Yet people also need ways of actively 'making' sense of themselves and of the world in which they dwell. If they have difficulty in doing so they may themselves signify this difficulty in different ways – for example through their speech and behavioural signs, or through body signals or symptoms. If they lose their ability to make sense of themselves and of the world around them they may seek help from a friend or counsellor, therapist or physician in 'sorting things out' or 'sorting themselves out'. Their desire is to 'make sense' of their experience of themselves and of the world. For most people, including many counsellors and therapists, however, 'making sense' of experience means finding new ways to signify this sense. A counsellor for example, may perceive the signs of emotion behind a person's words, and help them to signify their emotions more precisely or more fully – either in words or through bodily self-expression. Yet signifying something we feel or sense is not the same as what I will term 'sentience', by which I do not mean simply 'sensory awareness' but the capacity to directly feel or sense meaning or significance in what we are aware of. Sentience is not *signified sense* but *sensed significance* – what Eugene Gendlin has called "felt sense".

Gendlin points out that without felt sense it would be impossible for us to feel at a loss for words, to feel what we mean without yet having the words to express it. Nor would we be able to assess the 'fittingness' of our words and concepts, to sense whether or not they are truly in resonance with our own or other people's felt meanings or intents. But there is a deeper significance to the notion of felt sense or directly sensed significance. Generally, if someone talks about an experienced event or emotion, then they are seeking to 'make sense' of it by signifying it through words. But what is it that is actually signified by their words? Is it merely, as conventional semiotics would have it, some mental image or recollection of the emotions or events experienced? Or is it rather that through language we do not merely signify or 'refer' to specific events or emotions but seek to express the sensed meaning or significance that they hold for us?

Gendlin's semiotics of 'felt sense' challenges a number of basic ideas regarding the nature of signs belonging to the two most well-known theories of signs – those of Charles Peirce and Ferdinand Saussure:

- The Peircean assumption that signs 'stand for' or 'represent' some pre-given 'thing' or concept of that thing.

- The identification of the meaning or sense of the sign with its reference to some thing or idea of that thing – whether a fact or feeling, thing or thought, event or emotion.

- The Saussurean idea that the sense of a sign is reducible to its relation to other signs, its place within a larger sign system or pattern of significance.

- The assumption that the sense of a sign is something purely mental such as the thought, concept or image or memory that it evokes in our minds.

- The assumption that meaning or 'sense' is a *property* of 'signs' or 'sign systems' - rather than being an intrinsic dimension of sensory experiencing and phenomena as such.

What these semiotic superstitions have in common is that they themselves define a particular way of making sense of the world – that particular 'semiostructure' which defines our consensual reality. The world of consensual reality is a world of signified sense structured by conventionalised signifiers with standardised 'senses'. It is a 'semiostructure' which leaves no room for sentience – for that '6th sense' or 'felt sense' that constitutes sensed significance.

The semiotics of felt sense is based on the revolutionary understanding that a sign, any sign, is not essentially a signifier *of* some 'thing' – whether an event, emotion or experienced reality of any sort. Instead the latter are themselves signs. As such, however, they are bearers of a directly felt or sensed meaning that transcends their conventional signification. Conventional significations have to do with the way 'one thing points to another', as for example, a road sign may point to a supermarket. Indeed the root meaning of the word 'sense' is a 'way' or 'direction'. But just as a road sign does not essentially point to a thing – the supermarket – but points us to its direction, so is the essential meaning or 'sense' of any sign a direction of awareness. Sensing the significance of a sign does not mean interpreting what it signifies, looking for some 'thing' that it points to. It means letting our own awareness be directed by it in a specific way. The meaning of a person's body language – a look in their eyes for example – lies not in something they are looking at but in the way of looking at and seeing that thing. The look in their eyes reveals the character of their gaze, which is not an object, internal or external, but a direction of awareness toned and coloured by a particular mood or mode of awareness.

In the semiotics of felt sense, meaning or significance is not seen as a property of signs at all – whether road signs, words, body signals, dream symbols or physical symptoms. For whilst felt sense can be carried over or communicated through signs and through the word (*dia-logos*), it is not something that can be defined in words or reduced to some 'thing' that a sign points to.

The sensed significance of a sign always transcends its conventional or signified sense. Though the signified sense of a red traffic light signal is 'stop', the felt significance of having to stop, here and now, at this traffic light, on this particular journey, undertaken for this particular end, in the particular context of their lives, will be quite different for every person who stops at the signal. More seriously, a patient's symptoms may be taken by a physician as a sign in the conventional sense – taken as signifying or pointing to some 'thing' such as a possible organic 'disease'. Alternatively, however, both the sign and the supposed 'thing' to which it points may be taken as something that directs the physician's awareness in such way as to give them a direct sense of the patient's felt dis-ease. Similarly, a dream symbol may be taken by a psychoanalyst as a sign of some other 'thing' – a repressed drive or desire for example. But in interpreting it in this way, the psychoanalyst, like the physician, is merely locating a sign within a conventionalised structure of signification – treating one thing as a sign that merely points to another. When the analyst interprets dream symbols, or when the analysand 'free associates' around them, what they come up with are but further symbols – further signifiers in a chain of signification. Medical diagnosis and psychoanalytic interpretation consist in 'explaining' one sign as the signifier of another. The bodily symptom is taken as a sign of an organic disorder. The dream symbol is taken as a sign of an unconscious wish or desire. The question of what the disorder or desire may itself be a symbol of is reduced to a question of its physical 'causes' or psychological 'repression'.

The sensed meaning of a poem, painting or piece of music can in no way be reduced to the words with which we represent it or to some 'things' it depicts. Similarly, the sensed significance of a dream symbol or body symptom, indeed of any phenomena we may be aware of, is, in contrast, not reducible either to a set of verbal signifiers, or to some 'thing' that they are taken to signify.

Sensed significance is not itself any 'thing' we are aware of, but rather consists of sensed patterns and qualities of awareness as such. A good example is music. The meaning we are aware of in the richly textured tone-colours of a symphony lies in the patterned harmonic textures, tones and colourations *of* awareness that the music itself expresses. The music can 'evoke' feelings through its tones and textures only because it is the resonant expression of patterned harmonic tones and textures *of* feeling. Its meaning does not lie in the thoughts or images it evokes, for these too, merely give actual or manifest form to the different potential patterns of significance sensed as feeling tones.

Both the sensed significance of words and the inner meaning of musical tones lie in their wordless inner resonances. Indeed the same can be said regarding the sensed significance of all sensory phenomena. Thus an infant does not hear a sound as that of a 'car passing by' or 'a clock ticking', for cars and clocks are 'things' we can signify in words only by virtue of their place within the conventionalised structure of signification that constitutes the adult world. For the infant, the sounds it hears are not the sounds of some pre-given 'things' such as cars or clocks. Rather what these things themselves 'are' and 'mean' for the infant *is* the particular way the infant senses them sounding and resounding within their field awareness.

True sentience relies on inner resonance. The importance of this in psychotherapy cannot be underestimated. To mentally register through some outward sign, a word or body signal for example, that a person is in a certain type of pain or distress, or that they are experiencing a specific emotion such as sadness or guilt, is one thing. But to attune to the felt, bodily sense of the specific 'mood' or 'tonality' of this person's pain or distress, this person's sadness or guilt, is quite another. Registering and 'reading' signs is the basis of emotional 'empathy'. Attunement to *felt sense* is the basis of what I call *felt resonance*.

The semiotics of felt sense is of no small theoretical significance. It points to a fundamental paradigm shift in the practice of both psychotherapy and somatic medicine. For paradoxically, the very attempt on the part of psychotherapists, psychoanalysts or physicians to 'make sense' of a client's experience and find out what their problems 'really' are turns into an attempt to reduce their felt sense of its significance to one 'central' or 'basic' signifier among others – identified according to the semiotic framework of their own professional training, theoretical models and practices.

From a soma-semiotic point of view, felt sense is an attunement to potential patterns of significance. The latter are in turn the source of all manifest or actual patterns – including linguistic patterns, mental patterns of thought, emotional patterns, existential or 'life patterns' and patterns of experienced events of all sorts. Gendlin points out that people tend to refer back to their unformulated felt sense of particular dimensions of their experience only when they are at a loss for words or do not know how to respond to a situation. The real reason *why* attending to felt sense helps us find appropriate words or responses that express what we mean is that through felt sense we attune to a field of awareness consisting of those potential patterns of speech and action which are the source of all actual patterns that we might embody and express.

Not just our own words or deeds but all experienced events are themselves actualised or manifest patterns of significance emerging from a field of potential or unmanifest patterns. That is why they possess an intrinsic sense that we can feel directly. Both language and experienced events give outer, phenomenal form to these patterns, and in doing so function as phenomenal signifiers of these patterns. The importance of talking specifically of signifiers of felt sense is that they include more than just words. A dream symbol or bodily symptom, life situation or event is also a signifier, giving manifest form to particular potential patterns of significance – but leaving other potential patterns unmanifest. That is because any phenomenal signifiers – any actualised pattern of speech or action, thought or emotion, emotions or experienced events, can give form to only one potential field pattern of significance. In doing so it leaves other patterns unmanifest – unperceived, unspoken, unthought. Were it not for felt sense, these unmanifest patterns would remain also unsensed and unfelt, for felt sense is also our awareness of the 'excess' of potential meaning or significance that no phenomenal signifier can ever express.

Our felt sense of the excess and unmanifest significance of experienced phenomena – objects or events, people, situations or words – is treated as something merely 'subjective', or as some dubious 'sixth sense' belonging to the realm of the extraordinary and paranormal. And in a certain sense this is right, for felt sense *is* our 'sixth sense' – but one that is the hidden basis of all others. For our five senses are what give manifest, experiential form to that source field of potential patterns of significance which felt sense links us to. However, signifiers of any type, whether verbal or experiential, not only give expression to felt sense but also enframe it in a particular way, giving form to certain potential field patterns of significance and leaving others unformed and unformulated. The result, unfortunately, is an entire culture and civilization in which meaning *as such* is identified not with intrinsically meaningful dimensions of the world, but only with formal signifiers that 'refer' to things in the world – such as words or visual signs, mental images or mathematical signs, scientific diagrams or observational 'data', religious symbols and scriptures etc. In other words meaning is seen primarily as a *property or function* of language and sign-systems. Experience and its sensed significance – sentience - is placed in a secondary role as that which is 'signified' by these sign-systems. The relation between language, lived experience and felt sense can be visualised in the form of an inverted triangle.

Diagram 1

signified sense
(manifest or actualised patterns of significance)

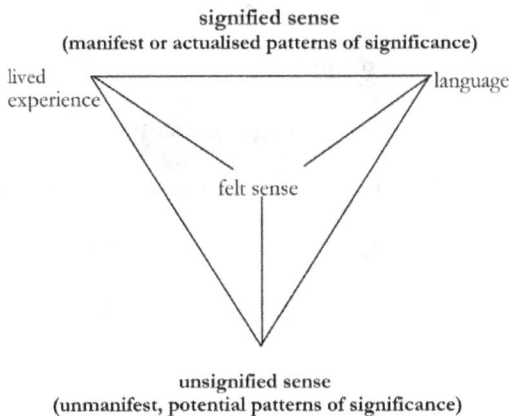

lived experience   language

felt sense

unsignified sense
(unmanifest, potential patterns of significance)

Conventional semiotics understands language as a sign system whose main role is to refer to, represent or 'signify' experienced events. Meaning or sense is identified with manifest or signified sense – verbal signifiers and the experienced reality they represent or refer to. But as the poet knows well, language can only truly do justice to our experience of the world if it is in resonance with felt sense – if it helps to give form to unformulated or unmanifest patterns of significance that are always latent in experienced reality itself. Felt sense is our link with the unsignified meaning of experienced events – with those potential patterns of signification that are the source of all actual patterns of experience and language. If we see the purpose of language as one of giving some sort of literal account of experienced reality, we ignore its true role – which is to confirm and agree on the 'reality' of whatever actual pattern of significance it was by which we first made sense of experienced events and emotions. But language can serve another function too, that of giving expression to our felt sense of different potential patterns of significance – those patterns that we chose not to actualise in our experience, and therefore have difficulty describing in words. If this function of language is ignored, felt sense is sacrificed to signified sense and language is reduced to the status of a set of conventional patterns of signification designed to affirm a consensual reality – a set of agreed patterns of significance within our experience. Unless they become artists of one sort or another, those whose modes of experiencing or expression fall outside these ordered patterns of signification or sense-making may be regarded either as mystics – or else as suffering from some sort of mental disorder, and in need of psychiatric help or psychotherapy.

The Semiotics of Felt Sense in Psychotherapy
... from signified sense to sensed significance

The semiotics of felt sense marks a fundamental paradigm shift in the focus of psychotherapy:

- From 'feelings' and their 'meanings', to directly felt meanings or 'felt sense' as such.

- From expressing feelings through signifiers to directly *feeling* what it is they signify.

- From meanings or senses that are verbally signified and enframed in words to those that are felt or sensed in a wordless, bodily way.

- From facts or feelings to the felt meaning or 'sense' of those facts or feelings.

- From *signifying feelings* in words and body signals to *feeling their significance.*

- From *signified senses* to *sensed significances*.

- From a focus on some signified 'thing' that a client's verbal signifiers might signify or refer to, to a focus on the way signifiers give form to felt meaning or sense.

- From the *eclipse or foreclosure* of felt sense through being given form in linguistic and phenomenal signifiers, to its *resonant amplification* through those signifiers.

- From the *therapist's* felt sense of a client's body signs and verbal signifiers to a felt *resonance* with the client's own sense of their significance.

Up until now, however, psychotherapy in the form of the so-called 'talking cure' has been dominated by what could be called semiotic reductionism. The therapist listens to a client's linguistic account of experienced events, thoughts and emotions and responds in language. Though it may be understood (as in cognitive behavioural therapy) that a client's emotional responses to an experienced event may be shaped by their own linguistic or 'cognitive' interpretation of it, what is not generally understood is that the very phenomena which thought and verbal signifiers are a cognitive or communicative response *to* are themselves *signifying* phenomena – signifiers rather than signifieds – belonging as they do to particular *patterns of significance* which serve to give some sort of familiar order and structure to the patient's reality. If a client is unable to 'make sense' of an event or experience in terms of such familiar patterns of significance, therapists see their role as helping them to do so – and in this way to re-establishing a safe and ordered reality. One way of doing this is by looking for a different *pattern of significance* in the client's experience itself, and seeking to arrive at a consensual agreement with the client on the nature of this pattern.

The self-defined role of psychotherapists and counsellors in other words, is essentially to help the client to find patterns of significance already present in their lived experience whilst at the same time giving expression to what may be as-yet *unsensed* dimensions of this experience, and/or as-yet *unformulated* patterns of significance within it. In practice this task is often reduced to one of simply registering the linguistic signifiers and reading the bodily signs of a client's feelings, and then either re-framing them in terms of other words and signifiers or helping the client to do so. Yet helping a client to *signify* or 'express' feelings is not the same thing as *feeling* the sense or significance of those signifiers – or helping the client to do so. This demands attention to what Gendlin calls 'felt sense' i.e., to the realm of directly *sensed significance* rather than its translation into already *signified senses* of language and other signifying phenomena.

Yet in the current practice of counselling and psychotherapy, what Gendlin calls 'felt sense'. i.e. *pre-linguistically* sensed significance is all too easily eclipsed - enframed and foreclosed - by linguistically signified senses. Thus no sooner does a client – or therapist – become aware of a felt, bodily sense of something significant, then the temptation is to immediately enframe this pre-linguistically sensed significance in words – words which carry with them the baggage of their own *already-established and signified senses*. The danger here is not only that the original pre-linguistic sense is distorted by the very language in which it is expressed and enframed, but also that it is wholly *eclipsed and foreclosed by* that translation. This foreclosure or eclipse of felt, bodily sense prevents both therapist and client from checking out and refining their own linguistic 'translation' by referring back to the original pre-linguistic sense that was its source. It was Gendlin's chief observation that those clients who benefited most from therapy were those most aware of and most capable of patiently staying with or 'focussing' on their direct felt, bodily sense of 'dis-ease'. Such clients were able also to go through the various stages that Gendlin came to define as an innately therapeutic practice of 'Focusing'.

Gendlin writes of and teaches 'Focusing' as a *self-therapeutic* process by which anyone can be encouraged to attend to or 'focus' on their immediate, bodily felt sense of their current state of being - only *then* letting mental signifiers (words or images) arise which give form to or provide a "handle" on this felt sense. He describes the next stage of the Focusing process as one of "resonating back and forth" between a given word or image and the felt sense that is its source. If the word or image is a genuinely fitting one - in full *resonance* with the felt sense from which it arose - this resonance will itself be felt and sensed in an immediate bodily way – resulting in what Gendlin calls a *felt shift* in our directly sensed, bodily state of being. Yet this vital process of "resonating back and forth" between mental signifiers and felt sense in order to check out the fittingness of the former is impossible if, as so often happens, words and images arise in a person's mind *without* a prior awareness of the felt bodily sense that is their source. It is *also* impossible if, as I believe so often happens in the therapeutic process, mental signifiers – not just those of the client but also those of the therapist, analyst or counsellor - tend to immediately *enframe and foreclose* the felt, bodily sense that is their source, thus leaving no time-space for alternative, more fitting or 'resonant' signifiers to arise from it.

Unfortunately the entire framework of psychotherapy and counselling training encourages such a premature foreclosure and enframement of felt sense, dominated as it is by the belief that the therapist's *listening process* is merely a *prelude* to providing some form of verbal response to the client - one whose sole *purpose* is to translate felt sense into verbal signifiers. Deep listening on the other hand is not merely about cognitively 'making sense' of what one hears, but becoming 'all ear' - using one's whole *body* to directly *sense* its significance. Nor it is a mere prelude to verbal response but a way of entering into a state of wordless inner *resonance* with another. Only by listening with our 'third ear' - our directly felt, bodily sense of another person's words and body language – and through such a state of wordless resonance, can one find responsive words that are fully in resonance *with* the other. And only language in full *resonance* with felt, pre-linguistic sense will not enframe and eclipse it - reducing it to some stereotyped pattern of linguistic signification. Instead it will *amplify* felt sense, and in this way also help one to stay in touch with it. This capacity to stay in touch with felt sense is also the condition for transforming it into a felt *resonance* with a client's own as yet unformulated sense of the inner meaning or significance of the events and emotions they experience – thus putting the client themselves more in touch with felt, bodily sense.

Deep *bodily* listening on the other hand is a listening which facilitates the transformation of felt sense not only into fully resonant signifiers, but also into felt resonance with another person. Both these forms of resonance amplify felt sense. Yet many of the theoretical frameworks on which psychotherapy and counselling are currently based are a substitute for a deeper understanding of listening as such – not as a mere prelude to some form of therapeutic verbal response but as an attunement to felt sense and a medium of wordless resonance with the client. Similarly, many therapeutic and counselling relationships are a substitute for deep, listening in social relationships in general – not least the client's own relationships with others outside the therapeutic relationship. The soma-semiotics of felt sense and felt resonance is therefore of fundamental importance for the training of psychotherapists of all sorts, stressing as it does the fundamental character of listening as a whole-body activity – a form of *whole-body sensing* or 'soma-sensitivity' naturally attuned to sensing meaning or 'sense' as such in an immediate, bodily way. In this way soma-semiotics and soma-sensitivity provides the missing link between psychotherapy, on the one hand and somatic medicine on the other, allowing the therapist to attune to a patient's felt body, felt self and felt sense of 'dis-ease' - one which can just as well find expression in somatic symptoms and 'disease' as in disturbances to their mental-emotional life and behaviour.

According to the biologist Rupert Sheldrake, the biological form (*morphe*) of any organism is stabilised and maintained by *resonance* with its own underlying organising pattern or 'morphic field'. Yet Sheldrake's key term for this process - "morphic resonance" - can also be used to describe the process by which *linguistic* forms or patterns of signification are stabilised by resonance with the *pre-linguistic* field patterns of significance they give form to. For what Gendlin calls 'felt sense' is also a type of 'field sense' - an attunement to latent or underlying field patterns of significance that remain as-yet *unfelt, unformed and unformulated.* Both the power of language to entrap and eclipse, enframe and foreclose felt sense *and* its potential to give resonant form to felt sense - thus amplifying and transforming it - are, in this sense, expressions of 'morphic resonance'.

Language does not only 'express' meanings – understood as pre-linguistic patterns of significance - but can also eclipse other potential meanings or patterns of significance. The *eclipse* of felt sense arises because, through the process of 'morphic resonance', selected patterns of significance are *stabilised and reinforced* through resonance with particular patterns or modes of linguistic expression – yet at the expense of giving resonant form to other *pre-linguistic* patterns of significance that thus remain unfelt and unformulated, lacking truly resonant linguistic signifiers.

Only through felt sense can we stay in touch with such unformed or unsignified senses and the patterns of significance they conceal. And a truly 'resonant' signifier – 'the fitting word' - is one that gives form to felt sense without foreclosing it – and in this way give form to or formulate particular patterns of significance without eclipsing as-yet unformed or unformulated ones. A truly 'resonant' linguistic response or 'interpretation' is one that formulates certain felt patterns of significance whilst at the same amplifying rather than foreclosing our still unformulated, feeling sense of other *potential* patterns of significance. Yet both 'Focusing' and morphic resonance are not merely intra-personal processes and dynamics but also have profound inter-personal, inter-subjective and inter-bodily dimensions - offering a gateway to a more deeply felt sense of and resonance with others.

When Gendlin writes of the role of 'felt sense' and the 'Focusing' process in psychotherapy, he sees the role of the therapist purely as that of helping the client to Focus themselves i.e. to go through the stages of attending to their bodies - their chest and belly in particular - focusing on the wordless tones and textures of bodily feeling they experience there, letting these take shape in words and images and then 'resonating' back and forth between these mental signifiers and the felt sense that is their source until a 'felt shift' occurs (a shift that I see not just as an alteration in 'felt sense' but in what I call the 'felt body' and 'felt self'). What Gendlin does not fully address or explore however is the potential *relational* dimension of 'Focusing' in the context of psychotherapy as usually practiced - where the issue is not only the *client's* capacity to be aware of, attend to and 'Focus' on felt sense - but also that of the therapist's capacity to do so. For if the latter too is capable of staying with their own bodily, felt sense of a client's dis-ease, then this sense can become a gateway to a *felt resonance* with the client of a sort that is intrinsically healing.

The following diagrams seek to represent the missing relational dimension of Focusing by showing how the soma-semiotics of 'felt sense' operates in a bi-personal or dyadic field – in particular that constituted by the relationship of therapist and client.

Diagram 1 represents the fundamental soma-semiotic matrix that constitutes the dyadic field of self and other. The upper field of the matrix is the domain of *signified sense* or 'signification' (SIG). This is the realm, not only of verbal or linguistic signifiers but of all phenomena that address us, speak to us and hold meaning for us - and are in this sense also signifiers with the character of a language. This includes specific events and situations, thoughts and emotions, dreams, mental images, body signals and somatic symptoms – all of which constitute languages in their own right – expressed as manifest *patterns of significance*. The lower field is a domain of *sensed significance* (SEN). This is the realm of pre-linguistic patterns of significance, made up of potential signifiers and signifying phenomena of a sort that can only begin to take form through attention to unformed sensed or bodily 'felt sense'. The dotted line represents the demarcation line of these two realms, and also their dynamic relation.

Diagram 1

SIG	manifest or actual patterns of signification	SIG

Self   SIGNIFIED SENSE (SIG)   Other

SENSED SIGNIFICANCE (SEN)

SEN   unmanifest phenomena and patterns of significance   SEN

This dyadic field can of course be seen specifically as the specific relational field of interaction between a therapist of any sort (physician, psychotherapist, counsellor or psychoanalyst) and their patient, client or analysand).

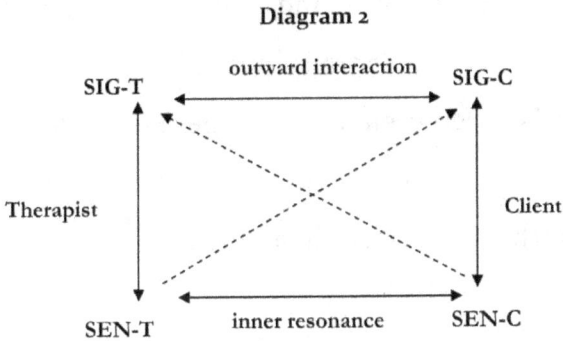

Diagram 2

```
                    outward interaction
      SIG-T                              SIG-C


    Therapist                            Client



      SEN-T      inner resonance         SEN-C
```

Here the vertical lines represent, for both therapists (T) and client (C), the dimension of *intra-subjective* resonance (or lack of it) between their signifiers and signifying patterns of speech and body language on the one hand, and the felt sense that is their source. The bottom horizontal line represents the potential for direct *inter-subjective* resonance (or lack of it) between therapist and client on the pre-linguistic level of felt sense and the felt body and self. The topmost line represents the degree to which this is reflected in the outward interaction, linguistic and bodily, of therapist and client. Finally, the dotted diagonal lines constitute a semiotic representation of what in psychoanalysis would be referred to as dynamics of 'transference' and 'counter-transference i.e., the way in which the client's felt senses, felt self and felt body seek and find a reflection in the therapist's signifiers ('transference') and, conversely, the way in which the therapist's felt senses, self and body find expression in the client's signifiers ('counter-transference').

Diagram 3 is a representation of the basic relational pattern which, I believe, much psychotherapy training encourages – a pattern nevertheless *deficient* in a fundamental way.

Diagram 3

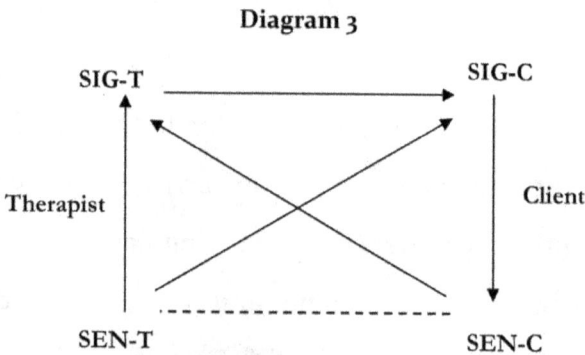

Here the one-way arrow from SEN-T to SIG-T represents the way in which a felt sense is no sooner registered than eclipsed by its expression in words and other signifiers. In other words it represent a lack of the necessary *intra-subjective* resonance on the part of the therapists through which they are able to retain, refer back to and resonate back and forth between their own felt sense and the signifiers that give form (*morphe*) to it – checking to see whether these are in full *resonance* with felt sense ('morphic resonance'). The one-way arrows from SIG-T to SIG-C and thence to SEN-C represent the danger of the therapist's signifiers being taken up by the client in a way which shapes or distorts their own felt sense, felt body and felt self – without necessarily being in resonance with them. The bottom dotted line represents the lack of direct *inter-subjective* resonance on the level of felt sense which results from (a) the intra-subjective eclipse of felt sense by the therapist in the very act of its transformation into formed signifiers, and (b) the *intra-subjective* enframement or distortion of the client's own felt sense through signifiers influenced by those of the therapist. It is precisely such lack of direct *inter-subjective* resonance on the level of felt sense - of pre-linguistic, bodily sensing – that the 'unconscious' dynamics of 'transference' and 'counter-transference' compensate and substitute for. For the 'unconscious' nature of these dynamics has to do with the fact that the diagonal arrows indicating them are also 'one-way' – leading from the realm of felt sense to that of formed signifiers and yet eclipsing direct awareness or 'consciousness' of the felt body and felt sense in this very process.

The missing dimensions of both intra-subjective and inter-subjective relationality in Diagram 3 are brought to the fore in

Diagram 4

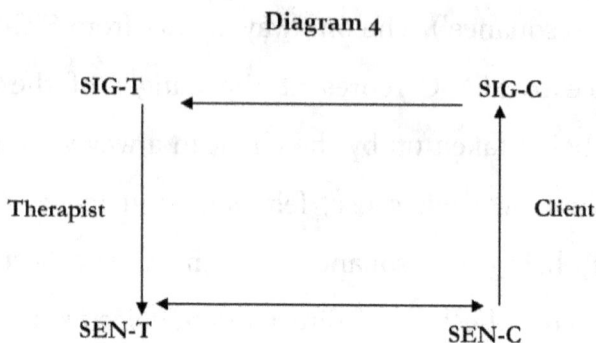

Here the arrow SIG-C to SIG-T suggests a mode of interaction in which the therapist is somatically receptive and sensitive to the signifiers of the client and (as indicated by the arrow from SIG-T to SEN-T) seeks precisely to use their capacity for pre-linguistic bodily sensing or 'soma-sensitivity' to attain a felt sense of their meaning *for* the client. If successful, this will result in a state of inter-subjective resonance between therapist and client at the level of felt sense, one that in turn will allow the emergence of richer and more intra-subjectively resonant signifiers in the consciousness of the client (the arrow SEN-C to SIG-C).

The failure to distinguish the domains of *felt sense* and its *signifiers*, between *signified sense* and *sensed significance* and the resonant - or dissonant - relation between them, is reflected in a failure to acknowledge a whole range of parallel distinctions. These include the fundamental failure of biomedicine to distinguish between the felt body (the body as felt from within) and the 'physical' body (the body as perceived from without) and between symptoms as 'signs' of some objective organic disease or as *expressions* of a subjectively felt dis-ease. For 'expression' or 'signification' is, in principle, something fundamentally distinct from 'causation' - even so-called 'psycho-somatic' or 'psychogenic' causation. The signification of felt bodily sense finds expression in signifying phenomena or 'signifiers' of all sorts - whether in the form of words or mental images, thoughts and emotions, dream or waking life events, and/or or somatic symptoms. Hence the significance of what I term 'soma-semiotics', not just in the practice of psychotherapy but in rethinking its role in addressing *dis-ease* in all its expressions – including somatic illness.

The Semiotics of Felt Sense in Somatic Medicine

...from psychosomatics to soma-semiotics

The term 'bio-logy' refers to the speech or language (*logos*) of life (*bios*). Of fundamental significance to biology is the understanding of life itself *as* a language. It was the German biologist Jakob von Uexküll who inaugurated what was later to be called a 'biosemiotic' understanding of living organisms. His radical insight was that each species of animal or organism dwells in its own unique sensory environment (German *Umwelt* or 'surrounding world'). This unique *subjective environment* is not shaped by the organism's sense organs alone but by the *sensed significance* it attaches to different sensory 'cues'. Thus within the sensory environment of a tick, for example, unlike within that of human beings, there is *simply no such thing* as a rabbit, rat, cow or sheep. Instead there is simply the smell of mammalian sweat, and the tactile sense of mammalian hair and skin warmth. Whereas for the human species therefore, 'mammalian' is merely a *generic concept* (signifying a genus of sub-species perceptible in our environment) within the sensory environment of the tick 'mammalness' is a dimension of *immediately sensed significance*. It *enacts* this sensed meaning or significance through dropping from a tree onto a mammal, letting itself be guided by its hair towards its skin, and then using heat cues to begin sucking blood - which it neither sees nor tastes.

The surrounding environment or *Umwelt* of the organism therefore constitutes a unique *sign-world* or 'semiosphere'. The body of the organism is a medium of motoric response to cues coming from this sign world – and in this way a medium of active 'signification' or 'sign-making' which in turn *alters* that world. For example the act of dropping from a tree and finding itself on the hair or skin surface of a human are both an *enactment* and a consequent *alteration* of the principal cues or signs that constitute the immediate sensory and sign world of the tick.

From the perspective of Uexküll's 'environmental theory' the very term 'environment' cannot be taken as referring to a singular reality –each organism dwelling as it does in its own unique and species-specific sensory environment. The life of the organism in its own environment is essentially a *semiotic circle* shaped by (a) the particular phenomena it experiences in its own environmental field of sensory experiencing (b) the selective sense that it makes of those phenomena and (c) the motoric responses through which it enacts that sense, and (d) the way these enacted senses in turn both *alter* the organism's sensory environment and constitute *signifying acts* for other organisms within that environment (for example a human being who recognises a localised skin sensation of pain as the actual or potential sign of a tick having lanced their skin).

For Uexküll, as for Heidegger, the 'subjectivity' of an organism is not that of a 'subject' or 'I' experiencing an 'objective' environment shared with other species. Instead the subjectivity of any organism is constituted *by* its unique subjective *world* – a world of *directly sensed significance*.

Whereas Uexküll recognised the organism's entire sensory world or environment as an immediately sensed and living sign-world comparable to a language, molecular reductionism identifies the 'language of life' only with its expression in a genetic 'alphabet' or 'vocabulary'. In this way, as Heidegger noted, a reduction is performed. Significant communication "is reduced to a mere series of reciprocal releasing mechanisms" between chemical molecules, whilst at the same time "chemical processes are elevated to linguistic communication".

Since meaning-full *experiencing* (*Er-leben*) is the sensual essence of life (*Leben*) itself, neither 'experiencing' nor 'life' can be reduced to or 'explained' through the theoretical frame of 'biology' as a science. Thus the essence of biology, is, as Heidegger remarked, nothing 'biological' in the scientific sense. Instead it is quite literally the word (*logos*) of life (*bios*). 'Life' (*bios*) understood as 'word' or *logos* is essentially a sensual medium of *expression* of meaning or 'sense' - one whose most meaningful and primordial language is the language of immediate experiencing (*Er-leben*) as such. An authentically *biological* medicine therefore cannot rest on the reduction of the human body to a set of 'biosemiotic' processes reduced purely to processes of molecular 'information' exchange. Instead its focus must be on the patient's own *soma-semiotic* activity – their way of sensing and making sense of the signs coming from their environment or life world, the way in which the sense they make of these signs may in turn be both signified and sensed in the form of bodily symptoms and sensations of *dis-ease*. From a soma-semiotic perspective, so-called 'disease' symptoms and sensations are not taken diagnostically – as potential signs of an objective disease 'entity' in the form of bacterial or viral activity or the growth of a cancerous tumour. Instead such 'objective' diseases and their outward symptoms or signs are understood as symbols or signs of something else – a subjectively felt or sensed dis-ease of the individual human being in relation to their environment or life world. This dis-ease in relation to the individual's experienced life world however, is in turn inseparable from their experienced *sense of self.*

When we are ill we do not 'feel ourselves'. That is not because we are the victims of foreign bodies such as micro-organisms, toxins or antigens – what immunology and oncology describe as 'non-self' molecules or cells. Fundamental dis-ease, our 'not feeling ourselves', arises because we are on the way to 'feeling another self' – but have not yet found the way to embody and express that new sense of self.

What I call 'self-states' are *field states of awareness* with which we are completely *identified.* These field states of awareness are experienced as tonalities and textures of awareness, which, like moods, so completely permeate our felt sense of self and so colour our awareness of the world that we are hardly aware of them – unless they change. New field states of awareness however, may be initially experienced as threatening – in dissonance with an established sense of self, or in dissonance with mental and emotional patterns that express that existing sense of self.

What we call the 'self' has itself a field character, consisting of a unique range of self-states – uniquely toned intensities and colourations of awareness, bearing within them unique field patterns of awareness that shape our personal reality. Illness, dis-ease and dissonance are a natural part of the health process by which we learn to resonate with new aspects of our own larger identity or self-field. Illness is the bodily expression of dissonant organismic field states of awareness in which our beliefs and world picture distort our experience of new self-states and deny expression to them. They form part of a mental immune system whose function is not to protect our bodies from infection or colonisation by foreign bodies – so-called 'non-self' cells – but to protect our self-experience from infection by aspects of ourselves that we still experience as foreign or 'non-self'.

Our self-experience not only shapes and colours our experience of other people and the world, but is also reshaped and recoloured by it, allowing us to experience new aspects of ourselves, and to identify with new self-states or selves. In this way we grow as individuals, learning to give expression to new potentials latent within our own self-field, doing so through resonance with the self-fields of others and with their actual patterns of self-expression. Health, from this point of view, is not a continuous state of undifferentiated well-being, balance or harmony but a continuous process of change or metamorphosis, based on a balance of balance and imbalance, a harmony of resonance and dissonance through which we give expression to new psychic potentials of our inner being – our as yet unexpressed psychic genes.

Through respiration, circulation and metabolism, our bodies have no natural difficulty in absorbing foreign matter and reconstituting themselves from it. Our own inability to process the raw material of our experience, using it not only to reconstitute, but to recreate and reshape our selves from it – hinders and interferes with the organismic field patterns that shape and sustain our bodies' own respiratory, circulatory and metabolic patterns. Soma-semiotics understands physiological disorders as a precise symbolic expression of disorders of psychic respiration, circulation, metabolism and immune functioning. These in turn are the expression of a felt dis-ease which is the expression of dissonant field states of awareness – a lack of resonance with new and hitherto foreign field state of awareness that form part of our larger identity or 'self-field'. This lack of resonance with aspects of ourselves may be experienced initially as dissonances in our relationships with other people or our environment, as 'stress' induced by dissonances we experience in other people and our environment, or as 'cognitive dissonance' – beliefs that are in conflict with each other or with our own internally sensed environment.

Felt dis-ease is first and foremost a sense of muddied organismic field state or disordered organismic field patterns of awareness. Here, following Uexküll, it is vital to recognise that the nature of any life form or organism cannot be reduced to the way it is perceived by any *other* species of organism – shaped as this is by their own species-specific *field patterns of awareness* and the subjectively perceived environment or *patterned field of awareness* this creates. What any organism essentially *is* is a set of *organising field patterns* of awareness creating its own *patterned field of awareness* – its subjectively experienced life world, environment or 'Umwelt'. Field states of awareness are an expression of these organising field patterns of awareness. The latter in turn are stabilised through resonance with their manifestation as anatomical forms and morphological structures, mental and behavioural patterns, sensory and motor patterns, physiological and neurological patterns etc. This is my understanding of the new principle of life that Rupert Sheldrake has called 'morphic resonance' – the stabilisation of what he terms a 'morphic field' (i.e. an organising field pattern of awareness) through 'resonance' with its manifest biological form (Greek *morphe*).

Lack of resonance can result in felt dis-ease i.e. a muddied, hollow or discordant field state of bodily self-awareness – an 'unsound' state lacking a clear resonant tonality. That is why we speak of people 'sounding well' or being in 'sound' condition. Dis-ease can also arise from resonances or discordances between individual field states, field patterns and field tonalities of awareness and those manifest in a person's familial and social fields. When someone speaks of feeling socially 'stifled' or of having no 'room to breathe' this is not usually meant in a literal, bodily sense, but nor is it a 'mere' bodily metaphor. It is a description of a felt organismic state. Conversely, however if someone breathes more freely as a result of feeling their 'spirits' lift, then it is their actual bodily breathing that is the metaphor – a living, biological 'metaphor' of their inner being. A person can jog or exercise, or practice Yogic breathing exercises for hours, days or years without it significantly affecting their fundamental respiration – without it bringing new sources of spiritual meaning and inspiration into their lives. But a person can be neither spiritually inspired nor dispirited without it being instantaneously embodied in their physical breathing. The organism is the instrument with which we constantly translate states of being into mental and physical states, and transform basic capacities of our being into organic functions.

According to Martin Heidegger "We cannot say that the organ has capacities, but must say that the capacity has organs....capability, articulating itself into capacities creating organs characterises the organism as such."

Respiration, for example, is not merely an organic bodily function but the embodiment of a fundamental capacity of our being. That is the capacity to engage in a rhythmic exchange with the 'atmosphere' of our life world – 'breathing in' our own awareness of it, drawing meaning and inspiration from it, and in turn allowing our awareness to flow back out into it – whether as a simple exhalation of breath or as meaningfully shaped and toned exhalation, as speech. At what point does the air we inhale become a part of us? At what point does our exhaled air cease, not only to be a part of our bodies but a part of us? Whether we draw into our awareness a 'breathtaking' landscape or an 'idea', we feel moved to inhale and then exhale deeply. Why? Because breathing is the embodiment of our fundamental organismic capacity to fully take into ourselves our awareness of something other than self, and in turn allow that awareness to flow out again into the atmosphere or field of awareness linking us with the world. The words 'respiration, inspiration, aspiration etc.

come from the Latin *spirare* – to breathe – just as the Greek word *psyche* originally meant the 'breath' that vitalised an otherwise lifeless corpse (*soma*). To speak of the 'psychosomatic' dimension of breathing disorders such as asthma or of their 'psychogenic' causation misses the point. For in doing so we by-pass the fundamental question of what breathing as such fundamentally *is* – not merely as an 'organic' function of our body but as an organismic capacity of our being – the 'organismic' capacity to breathe in our awareness of all we experience in our life world.

Specific organic dysfunctions such as respiratory, circulatory, or digestive dysfunction are the manifestation of the relation between inner organismic capacities and their embodiment in organic functions – for example the relation between an individual's inner or psychical respiration or metabolism and their physical respiration or metabolism. Outer metabolism is the functioning of the body in digesting and metabolising foodstuffs. Inner metabolism is the individual's capacity to digest and metabolise their own experience of themselves and the world. Every experience of the self is an experience of something or someone other than self – whether another person, a piece of music, or a percept of any form. Conversely, every experience of something or someone other than self affects our self-experience. For, it is not the same self we experience washing up, being with a close friend or partner, engaging with another person professionally or participating in a social or mass event.

Interaction with the world and other people is a way of expanding our identity of felt sense or self-experience by incorporating elements previously perceived as 'other than self'. What I call the Mental Immune System (MIS) governs and regulates the relation between our experience of others and otherness and our self-experience, maintaining a more or less rigid or flexible, closed or permeable boundary between that which we experience as 'self' and that which we experience as 'not-self'. Over-active mental immune defences can stretch and ultimately weaken the body's own immune functioning. For by not 'letting things get to us' – not allowing our experiencing to alter our sense of self – we establish a rigid 'immune self'. As a result we create a situation in which it is our bodies that have to do the 'letting in' - becoming biologically vulnerable to antigens or so-called 'non-self' elements such as bacteria or viruses. The illness we may then contract however can in turn serve a healing purpose, forcing us to relax our inner immune system, the mental defences of 'the immune self', and offering us the rest time and opportunity to literally *incorporate* these 'non-self' elements – not just organismically but in our very sense of self.

Just as the body can incorporate 'foreign bodies' whilst maintaining its patterned integrity so can the self – being itself a boundless field of actual and potential patterns, qualities and states of awareness. Yet whilst the body stops growing at a certain age the self never does – needing not only to maintain a sense of identity but to *expand* that identity. It does so by accepting new field states of awareness as *self-states*, as new ways of experiencing self and world that are now shaped and coloured by a specific mood, tone or quality of awareness that was hitherto felt as unfamiliar or foreign.

Psychic and somatic dimensions of dis-ease are by nature both distinct and inseparable - the human organism itself being essentially a psychic body, that is to say a body of *awareness* whose organising field patterns, field qualities and field states are the foundation of physiological functioning.

Dis-ease is an immediately sensed field state of organismic or bodily self-awareness. Specific somatic symptoms however, are, from a soma-semiotic perspective, essentially somatic signs or 'signifiers' of a felt *organismic dis-ease* rather than signs of an 'organic disease'.

Biomedicine takes symptoms as potential signs of an underlying organic disease rather than as metaphorical signifiers of a felt, subjective sense of dis-ease. The physician's first act is to separate the patient as a human being from their subjectively felt dis-ease, and instead objectify the latter as symptoms or signs of some 'thing' lying behind them – a diagnosable 'disease entity' of some sort.

The therapeutic relationship of patient and physician takes the form of a 'We and It' relationship – the 'It' being the suspected disease or its symptoms - rather than what Buber called an 'I-Thou' relationship. Diagnosis is based both on the patient's verbal reports and on the results of examinations or tests. Yet both the patient's words or verbal signifiers and the somatic symptoms or signifiers they describe are treated as signs pointing to an underlying disorder or disease which constitutes their 'cause'. This is like looking for hypothetical organic 'causes' of a person's words or body language rather than seeking to understand their communicative and expressive meaning – what they are *saying* through them.

The human body is the fleshly three-dimensional text whose inner dimensions of meaning cannot be discovered through any internal physical examination or testing. Both the patient's words and the symptoms they describe are symbols or signifiers of a felt sense of dis-ease with many layers of meaning.

It was Freud who first introduced the concept of "organ speech" (*Organsprache*) as the speech of the unconscious.

Indeed, when he was 82 years old he formulated what he called the *second fundamental principle of psychoanalysis* – one whose implications have since been largely ignored. According to this principle, what is truly 'psychical' manifests itself *primarily* in what were previously considered merely as 'parallel' or 'concomitant' *somatic* phenomena.

What I term soma-semiotics understands all somatic or 'organic' states as essentially psychical states or field states of awareness – and vice versa. The human organism is not seen as anything essentially 'biological', except in the root Greek sense of this term – as the 'life speech' (*bios logos*) of the soul or *psyche*. What is termed the 'physical' body is understood as but the outwardly perceived form of the human psychical organism – its sensory image or sign (*semeion*) and its signifying speech or *logos*. The soul or *psyche* itself on the other hand, is not seen as some 'thing' encapsulated by the body or brain, but rather as the body itself – not the 'objective' physical body but the lived or 'felt body'. This the body as *subjectively* felt and experienced from within, and as such transcends the fleshly confines of our own skins – being the body of our lived, subjective experiencing and subjectively experienced life world as a whole.

In this framework it makes no sense to speak of the 'psychogenic' or 'psychosomatic' *causation* of organic disease.

For the true relation of *psyche* and *soma* is a *semiotic* rather than a causal one – to do with the biological *expression* and signification of the directly felt meaning or sense of our subjective experiencing and experiential life world.

Soma-semiotics therefore explores the relation between, on the one hand, the patient's immediate subjective or psychical sense of dis-ease (its directly *sensed significance*) and, on the other hand, the 'signifiers' through which this subjective sense of dis-ease finds expression.

These signifiers include both *somatic signifiers* in the form of symptoms and *verbal* signifiers of the sort that point to the *metaphorical* significance of those symptoms - for example verbal expressions such as feeling 'disheartened' by or unable to 'stomach' something.

Thus, as illustrated in Diagram 1, a *somatic symptom* such as indigestion can be seen as a *somatic metaphor* for a subjective sense of dis-ease rooted in the felt 'indigestibility' of an experienced event or emotion – this sense of indigestibility being expressed by *verbal metaphors* such as 'hard to stomach'.

Diagram 1

somatic signifier **metaphorical signification**   *verbal signifier* e.g. 'hard to stomach'

dis-ease eg. an experienced
event or emotion felt as
'indigestible'

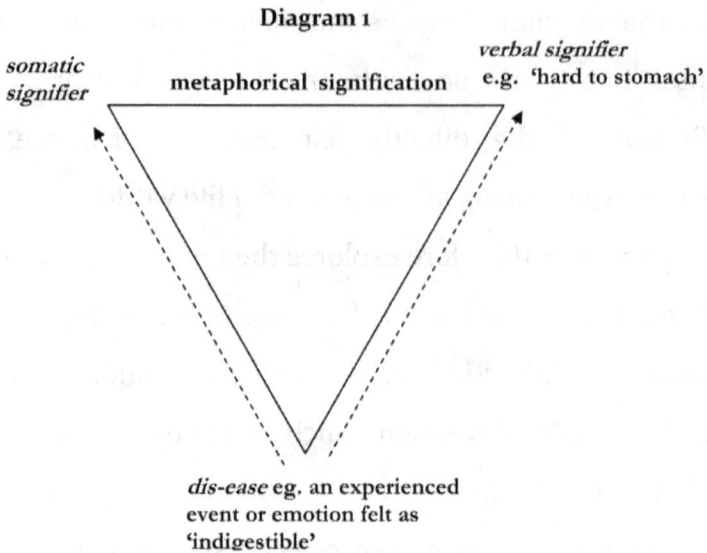

A disturbed capacity to digest experience in awareness – or receive the nourishment of meaning through it – results then in a disturbed organic capacity to digest food, not through a process of 'psychosomatic' or 'psychogenic' *causation,* but through a soma-semiotic process of metaphorical somatic *signification.*

In contrast Diagram 2 shows the way in which both patient and physician may understand the patient's speech only in a *literalistic* way – as signifiers 'representing' their symptoms – rather than understanding both the patient's words *and* the symptoms they signify as metaphors of a felt dis-ease. A patient, for example, may talk about heart symptoms without the physician taking either the word 'heart' or the heart symptoms themselves as metaphorical signifiers of an existential or emotional state of soul such as 'loss of heart'. Both patient and physician thus collude in (a) reducing the significance of the patients language to its literal *signification* in describing symptoms (b) interpreting the symptoms themselves as signs of an underlying disease 'entity' rather than as signifiers of a felt dis-ease, and (c) ignoring the role of the medical discourse and the media in *actively shaping both the somatic and verbal expression of that dis*-ease.

As a result, physician *and* patient effectively collude in reducing the patient's felt dis-ease to one or more symptoms capable of enabling the 'diagnosis' of a specific disease 'entity' such as cancer.

Diagram 2

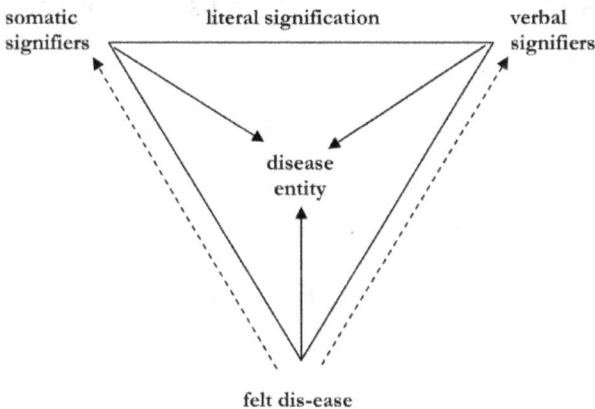

somatic signifiers   literal signification   verbal signifiers

disease entity

felt dis-ease

Diagram 2 also illustrates the 'pathological process' process by which a patient identifies with the suffering (Greek *pathos*) associated with a felt sense of dis-ease, and - encouraged by their physician - interprets the *somatic signs* or 'symptoms' of the latter as diagnostic signs of a pathological disease 'entity' or 'organic' pathology. Through this process the patient's own interpretation of their felt dis-ease begins to be *iatrogenically* distorted through biomedical diagnosis – the diagnosis itself being something that can induce fear and encourage further identification of the self with the state of 'being ill'.

Many writers on illness have instead emphasised the profound *metaphorical* significance of somatic symptoms and their verbal signifiers. Thus we can interpret the metaphorical significance of heart disease as an expression of 'disheartenment' or 'loss of heart', 'cold-heartedness' or 'heartlessness' or asthmatic symptoms as an expression of 'feeling stifled' or having 'no room to breathe'. The question arises however, as to why an experienced event or emotion should be experienced as psychically 'indigestible', 'stifling' or as an 'attack' on one's feelings or 'heart'. From a soma-semiotic perspective, the psychical *incapacity* to bear, breathe or digest elements of our lived experience is but the flip side of a latent psychical *capacity* to do so – a capacity which, if cultivated and exercised, would not only undermine the felt sense of dis-ease and render its somatic expression redundant, but also bring with it an altered sense of *self* – one no longer *identified* with the incapacity and its signifying symptoms.

Soma-semiotics thus reveals the intimate relation between what Gendlin calls 'felt sense' on the one hand, and what can be called the 'felt body' and 'felt self' on the other. Diagram 3 shows the *felt self* as the hidden centre of the triangle linking a felt sense of dis-ease to its metaphorical expression in both 'organ speech' and language, both somatic and verbal signifiers. The arrows represent a potential healing process by which the individual's felt dis-ease is allowed to alter and transform their self-state or sense of self, thus leading to a healthy change in the way this is somatically and verbally expressed.

Diagram 3

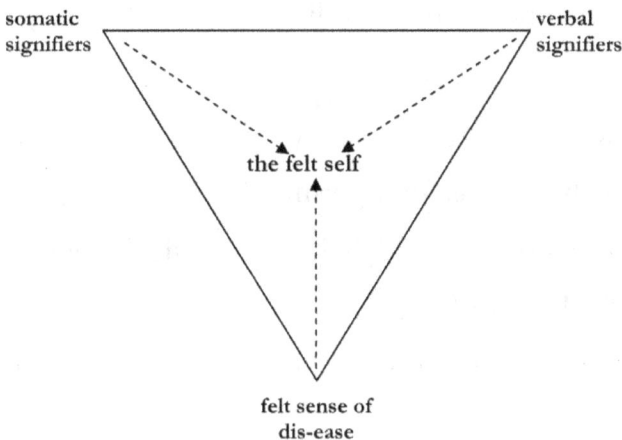

somatic signifiers

verbal signifiers

the felt self

felt sense of dis-ease

Many people who have successfully recovered from a serious state of ill-health do not simply 'feel themselves' again, but report feeling imbued with a *new* 'spirit' or sense of self. This confirms a new understanding of the essential *meaning* of illness - as that of helping us give birth to a *new* sense of self. This new 'felt self' is thus no mere by-product of the healing process but its very essence – that which overcomes the symptoms arising from the mental immune system and 'the immune self' – that self which seeks to *immunise* the individual from any changes in their felt self brought about through their experience of others and otherness.

Medically encouraged identification with sickness and a sick body goes along with identification of the *self* itself with a state of sickness – with a 'sick self'. Instead of understanding illness as a type of pregnancy through which the patient can give birth to and embody a new sense of self, it is as if pregnancy were taken as an illness.

Yet if the dominant medical metaphor is not one of 'illness as pregnancy' but rather of 'fighting' illness, 'war' against diseases or 'strengthening' the body's immunological 'defences' - and if both medical research and the media obsess themselves with the possible 'causes' and 'cures' of illness rather than their meaning -

then the production of *medically recognised* disease symptoms through a process of 'soma-semiosis' is actively *encouraged*.

The result will be an 'infection' of the patient through what used to be called a *miasma* – an unhealthy noxious 'atmosphere' or 'air' inducing fear or a mood of morbidity. The idea of miasmas or 'bad airs', emanating from swamps or marshes, as being responsible for infectious diseases is of course now seen as wholly outdated and 'unscientific' - having been totally replaced by the germ theory of disease. Yet the reality of 'miasmas' is nevertheless confirmed each time a new 'health' scare spreads through the *airwaves* of the media, pervading and infecting the general social *atmosphere* – whilst at the same time (in the case of flu scares for example) generating massive profits for pharmaceutical companies producing 'vaccines' for the next predicted pandemic.

There is always a natural aura or atmosphere or 'miasma' emanating from the patient's felt disease. This could offer the physician the means – through his or her own felt body – to directly sense and resonate with the patient's subjectively felt dis-ease. And yet what happens instead is that this dis-ease is amplified and distorted by the 'air' or 'atmosphere' – the *miasma* – generated by medical examinations, tests and diagnoses themselves. Indeed the patient's symptoms may already be a distortion of their dis-ease designed precisely to take the form of and receive acknowledgement as signs of a medically recognised disease pathology.

Biomedical diagnosis however, ignores the larger *context* of emergence of disease – its source in the patient's lived or felt body and in their life world as a whole. It does so because the *subjectively* felt dis-ease of the patient is not, in principle, capable of any form of *objective* medical examination, testing or treatment and nor is their *felt body* – which transcends the boundaries of their physical body and ultimately embraces their entire subjectively experienced world. The confusion between the *miasma* generated by the 'objective' biomedical diagnosis of disease and the miasma emanating from the patient's subjectively felt dis-ease is the principal obstacle preventing physicians from *using their own felt body* as the principal instrument by which to directly *sense* that dis-ease in and through its own *miasma* – essentially the bad air present in or pervading the patient's life world as a whole and the muddied, swamp-like tone of feeling *awareness* accompanying it.

Sensing the Patient's Felt Dis-ease

...from medical diagnosis to organismic resonance

Case Example 1

An elderly woman whose husband, Harry, has recently died from a heart attack finds herself suffering chest pains at night and goes to see her doctor. The physician is only interested in her symptoms as signs of a possible organic disorder which might be 'causing' them. He sends her to a consultant to test for possible heart conditions. Proving inconclusive, the consultant ends up diagnosing mild angina, and prescribes beta-blockers. These in turn prove to have little effect on the patient's symptoms. On visiting her doctor a second time however, the latter recalls her recent bereavement and, as a result, begins to read the somatic 'text' of her symptoms in a different way, understanding them in the life context of her loss and the pain it may be causing her. Rather than seeking a purely medical diagnosis of the patient's symptoms he himself listens to his patient in a genuinely patient and heartfelt way. Suddenly an insight flashes through his mind that constitutes a more fundamental diagnosis. He 'sees' that she may be suffering from a doubly broken heart "the one that killed Harry, and the one you're left alive with, that hurts when you're most alone in the middle of the night...the broken heart that gave up and the one that has to carry on painfully." The *heartfelt* hearing of the physician and the *heart-to-heart* talk that ensue may be the first time anyone has ever acknowledged *with and in their heart* the *heartache* of her loss. Yet this precisely is what gives her the *strength of heart* to acknowledge and bear it in a new way. The patient's heart symptoms disappear as metaphorical signifiers of her *broken heart*, not through an intellectual understanding of this significance but through a direct response from the inner heart of the physician – an exercise of his organismic capacity for heartfelt hearing.

This case vignette, presented by Dr David Zigmond in an article on different modes of patient-physician communication, goes to the very heart of the contrast between medical diagnosis and true *dia-gnosis*. The term 'diagnosis' means 'through knowing' (*dia-gnosis*). The Greek word *gnosis* derives in turn from the verb *gignostikein* – to 'know' in the sense of being *intuitively familiar or intimate with*. Gnosis is not knowledge 'of' or 'about' something, but the sort of knowing we refer to when we speak of knowing someone well or intimately. The relation that distinguishes this type of knowing is one in which, as Heidegger put it "we ourselves are related and in which the relation vibrates through our basic comportment". Medical knowledge, like other forms of scientific knowledge, including psychology, is knowledge 'of' or 'about' something. It represents the outer relationships between things or between people as if this were quite independent of our inner relation to them – our inner bearing towards them.

The change in the doctor's relationship to the patient in the second consultation was crucial. Rather than simply bringing to bear his medical-biological knowledge of the heart, he had the patience to bear with his patient – to acknowledge her heartbreak and bear it with her in a heartfelt way. As a result she no longer felt herself so painfully alone in bearing it, and was able as a result, to find a new bearing towards the loss that occasioned it. The paradox is that, despite the inconclusiveness of the medical tests, without adopting this bearing the patient might well have gone on to 'somatise' the pain of her lonely grief through increasingly acute symptoms, using them to feel and communicate it indirectly through a type of 'organ speech'. The GP's new bearing was preventative in the deepest sense, forestalling a process whereby this patient might well have ended up as a genuine 'heart case' requiring medical intervention or a 'heart sink' case in which no conclusive, measurable signs could be found of any organic disorder. When doctors speak of the 'heart-sink' patient perhaps all that is referred to is the type of patient that all too clearly needs this type of 'deep' fundamental diagnosis, rather than fruitless attempts to diagnose their symptoms in the ordinary way.

As Foucault puts it "To ask what is the essence of a disease is like asking what is the nature of the essence of a word." Our felt understanding of the sense or meaning of a word always has to do with connotations that transcend its given meaning or denotation. Just as the same words can have a different felt meaning to different people, so can the same disease symptoms. This felt meaning may not however be manifest, visible, or expressible. It belongs to the realm of unformulated experience. But for that which Foucault describes as 'the clinical gaze', what counts is only what is visible – manifest or expressible.

In Diagram 1 below the black squares represent outwardly manifest or expressible symptoms of the sort recognisable by physicians as potential diagnostic signs of a generic disease type.

The differently shaped figures *within* the two squares however, represent variations in the felt nature or 'shape' of two patient's inner, subjective experience of the same symptoms. The shaded area within these figures represents each patient's *felt dis-ease* as such – experienced as those specific qualities, tones and textures of *awareness* colouring both their subjectively felt body and their felt self and constituting not only a bodily state or condition but a *self-state*.

Diagram 1

 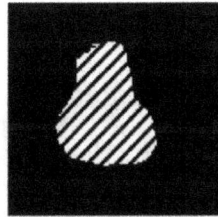

patient 1   patient 2

Diagram 2 is a model of the traditional "We-It" relationship between physician and patient, in which the physician's principle aim is to separate a patient's subjectively felt dis-ease from its medically-recognised disease symptoms, and turn the latter into a mutual "It" – a mere sign of some 'thing' that is 'wrong' with the patient and that can therefore be turned into an *object* of 'the clinical gaze' and of clinical diagnosis and treatment.

Diagram 2

patient   physician

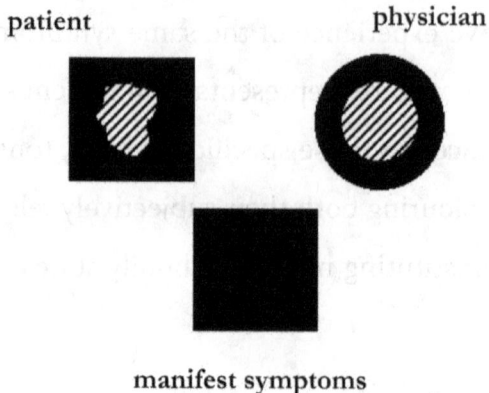

manifest symptoms

Diagram 3 represents the way in the patient's felt sense of dis-ease can itself take on the typical shape or pattern of a biomedically recognisable *disease* symptom – represented by a square. This may happen either because their symptoms are seen as signs of a specifically named disease by the physician and/or because a patient has themselves begun to interpret their felt dis-ease itself as the sign of an actual or potential disease, and to shape and share its physical symptoms accordingly - knowing that only in this way will they receive recognition of their felt dis-ease by the physician.

Diagram 3

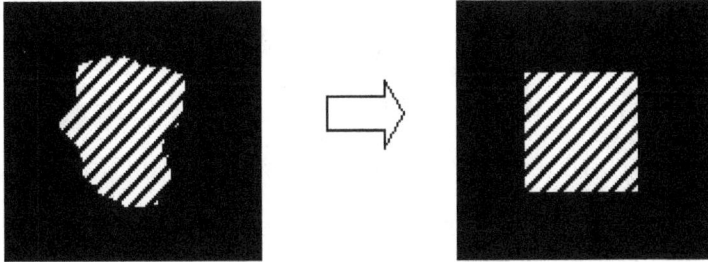

X-ray photographs, magnetic resonance scans and thermal imaging all show a different physical picture of the human body and brain. None of them however, can reveal anything of the individual's subjectively felt body and felt dis-ease – of those organising field qualities and patterns of awareness that constitute the subjective essence of all organisms – including the human organism. Nor do they show the role of beliefs about health and illness in shaping the organic and physical expression or signification of a felt, organismic dis-ease.

Whilst it is true that cognitive behavioural therapy, complementary medicine and the new field of psycho-neuroimmunology all offer accounts of how a person's beliefs can affect their bodily well-being, forging evidential or hypothetical links between 'mind' and 'body', none of these accounts distinguish the human 'mind' or 'body' on the one hand from the human organism on the other, or recognise both mental and physical states as the expression or embodiment of organismic states – field states of awareness that are at the same time 'self states' – bodily modes of self-experiencing.

Dis-ease is the experience of dissonant, degrading and/or newly emerging field states and self states of the human organism. Yet what we call the 'mind' is itself an integral part of the human organism, a body of thought-patterns or beliefs which actively shape and *in-form* organismic field states and can distort our felt sense of them in line with medical belief systems themselves. The patient dwells not only in a physical body but in a mental body of beliefs. The fundamental aim of the therapist should not be that of the conventional physician – namely to simply incorporate the patient's experience of ill-health into the mental body of beliefs that constitutes their particular brand of medical 'knowledge'. Rather, it should be to understand the patient's own body of beliefs, and its role in shaping their felt experience of dis-ease

Mental and medical bodies of belief constitute a type of social *text* inscribed into the very *texture* of the patient's felt, organismic experience of dis-ease - whilst at the same time ignoring its social and relational *context*. Thus a secretary, who feels abused and humiliated by her boss but incapable of facing up to him for fear of losing her job, develops instead an 'angry' skin rash on her face. The doctor or alternative practitioner she visits may know nothing of this situation and ask no questions that bring it to light. A diagnosis is made and treatment given which may or may not be effective. The greater danger, as in Zigmond's case study, is that the treatment is effective, for this may leave the patient with no option but to manifest or 'somatise' her dis-ease in another, perhaps more serious or life threatening way. All healing is fundamentally 'self-healing' in the deepest sense – allowing the very experience of illness to bring to awareness hitherto unmanifest and unfelt bodily 'self-states' – ways of being 'some body' and 'being a self' through which the individual is capable of meeting the challenges they face in their life world.

It is only through gaining a more detailed picture of the social and biographical background and current life context of a patient's symptoms that a therapist, guided by the principles of soma-semiotics, can begin to practice what can be termed 'organismic' healing. The first step on this road is to break with all forms of listening and diagnosis that are regarded as a mere *prelude* to some form of therapeutic response or medical diagnosis.

The second step on the road to organismic healing is the cultivation of a capacity for what I call 'soma-sensitivity' – leading to a state of 'somatic' resonance with the patient – what I call 'organismic resonance'. Somatic or organismic *resonance* is not the same thing as emotional empathy. We can register a sign of somatic discomfort or emotional distress in a person, and feel empathy or compassion for them, without in any way sensing with our own bodies the highly individual 'feeling tone' or 'field quality' of just *this* person's dis-ease, discomfort or distress, *this* person's pain or despair, this person's sadness or anger. Organismic resonance requires that the therapist use their own felt body as the principal instrument or *organon* with which to somatically sense and resonate with the patient's own organism and its felt dis-ease.

Healing begins and ends with being fully heard and felt as a human being. For the patient this means sensing that the therapist is listening with their body as a whole and not just with their head and mind, and that they are therefore able in some way to *feel* the way the patient does – capable of not just intellectually understanding or emotionally 'empathising' with the patient's experienced dis-ease but also sense it with and within their own subjective felt body - the organism.

The nature of organismic resonance between healer and patient was well summed up by a follower of Anton Mesmer.

"The nerves of the two human beings can be compared to chords of two musical instruments placed in the greatest possible harmony and union. When the chord is played on one instrument, a corresponding chord is created by resonance in the other instrument."

Tardy de Montravel

Diagram 4 represents a state of organismic resonance between patient and therapist through which the therapist has achieved a state of 'organismic identification' – i.e. gained a direct felt sense of the patient's own organismic field state and 'self state' within their own organism.

Diagram 4

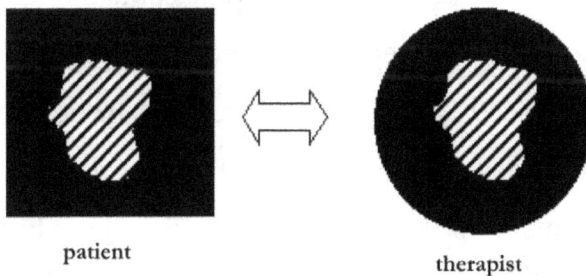

patient

therapist

'Organismic identification' is not the same as physical or emotional identification. For of course we cannot directly feel another person's physical pain or emotional state. What we *can* do however is to sense, resonate and identify with the unique qualitative 'tone' or 'mood' of their pain or emotions as these are sensed, expressed, emanated and communicated by the patient themselves in an immediate bodily way – as organismic states.

Case Example 2

A visibly stocky and muscular patient feels light or weightless to the therapist. Though she has a 'sunny' disposition, which can be sensed organismically as radiation of light and warmth it is as if her awareness were constantly streaming outwards towards the world and other people rather than inwards towards her own self. This was reflected in the fact that though she talked a lot about others and showed great emotional perceptiveness she never spoke directly about her own feelings or her experience of herself. A felt sense develops in the therapist of a hollow texture of the patient's inner bodily self-awareness – as if her awareness dwelled principally on the mental outer surface of her organism and was directed primarily towards her outer world - lacking any centre or core in its bodily, psychic interiority. Her sparkling eyes and talkative vitality betrayed a lacking depth and intensity in the patient's inner bodily self-awareness. Her awareness was so *outwardly* oriented, that it merged with her awareness of others and the world around her, as well as being restricted to and localised in her head rather than experienced with her felt body as a whole.

The therapist's direct organismic sense of the patient's bodily self-awareness – her felt body and self – was given significance by both her somatic complaints and the verbal information she shared. In a brief telephone call the therapist got an intuitive sense that the patient was in a sort of lonely existential vacuum. Later the patient reported that she was indeed alone in the house at the time, but also had, for a change, no external problems, her own or others, to distract her from the emptiness she felt within and around her in space. It was at this time that she experienced a somatic crisis in the form of an anaphylactic shock reaction in which her body tissues swelled, she felt like a balloon and due to constriction of her throat it became almost impossible for her to breathe or speak.

The therapist's organismic sense of the meaning of this crisis was that the patient's body was expanding to fill a vacuum created by the patient's lack of a rich and full *proprioceptive* sense of body and self. At the same time she was using the inflation and thickening of her physical body boundary to substitute for the otherwise unfelt boundary between self and other, self and world. This otherwise untrammelled, unmeasured and unidirectional flow of awareness from self to world - one through which she was always losing a bodily sense of self, was physically disrupted through her symptoms, making it almost impossible for her own breath to flow rhythmically in two directions - in and out. The allergic shock reaction in other words, was no mere response to a specific allergen, but rather her immune system compensating for a lack of boundedness in her organism and a lack of differentiation between self and other - one reflected in her language and way of speaking.

This is one example of an organic function (in this case the auto-immune function) compensating for a weak or non-existent psychical capacity to sustain a sealing organismic boundary or skin. As a result, her most continuous somatic symptom took the form of itchy skin eruptions which she scratched to the point of drawing blood – as if seeking to break into herself and find herself from the outside.

Further biographical questioning also revealed that in her childhood the patient had suffered from constant fears of her mother dying while she was at school – confirming the therapist's organismic sense of an absent differentiation of self and a significant other in the form of the mother. This too was related to the deathly quality of hollowness sensed in her felt body organism – which as a formative womb of awareness, has also the nature of a 'mother-body'. Lacking a safely containing and embracing organismic skin or 'amnion', fiery intensities of awareness arising from the core of the patient's self had neither a womb-like boundary to contain them or even expand within and rise to in the first place.

The patient's somatic sensation of intense bodily heat and going 'red in the face' during the somatic crisis allowed her inner fire to condense and rise to her physical skin surface rather than being dissipated in a habitual way through the friendly warmth and light of her sunny disposition. In contrast to this, a dream shared by the patient revealed an intense fear of darkness. Her predominant skin symptoms – hot and itchy eruptions – were also reminiscent of dark and bloody sunspots – being concentrations of heat on her skin surface that made her physically aware of a lacking organismic skin or boundary of awareness as such. This lacking organismic skin and sense of womb-like bodily self-containment was something she also made up for through a continuous mental skein and train of thoughts - all obsessively preoccupied with others rather than herself.

Therapy did not take the form of physical diagnosis and treatment, psychological explanations of symptoms or psychoanalytic interpretations focusing on emotional issues and their source in parent-child relationships. The fundamental therapy was the therapist's own 'soma-sensitivity' – his capacity to stay with his own felt, organismic sense of the patient's inner vacuum and lack of boundedness – despite all her surface vitality and talkativeness. This in turn induced a state of *resonance* with the patient's own organism – allowing *her* to feel its vacuum-like hollowness for the first time. The therapist then used his own organism to directly impart and induce a sense of inner warmth in the organism of the patient, helping her to feel her own body not as a vacuum emptied of awareness but as a womb-like vessel or hearth – filled with a warm glow of awareness stemming from her own life fire.

Just as there are organismic counterparts to every organ and physiological function (in this case the skin and auto-immune functions) so there are also inner subjective or 'psychical' counterparts to physical phenomena such as space and time, closeness and distance, warmth and coolness, light and darkness, lightness and heaviness, sound and density, charge and polarity, electricity and magnetism.

The organism as a subjective body is also composed of different 'elemental' qualities such as airiness, fluidity (water) and density or solidity (earth). Yet it is of the utmost importance not to confuse our felt sense of these qualities with bodily sensations of some physical or vitalistic 'energy'. Warmth of feeling or 'soul' is distinct in principle from physical heat and body temperature – even though the former might find expression in the latter. The warmth of feeling or soul we sense radiating from a human being is neither a measurable property of their physical body (temperature) nor some 'energy'. It is a quality of their own awareness of themselves and the world around them that others then feel bathed in and warmed by in their soul. And just as we can feel inwardly close to someone even though they may be many miles away in terms of physical distance, so can our feelings towards someone have a warm quality even though our bodies are freezing. Just as our organism, as a body of awareness, is not less but more fundamentally real than any physical phenomena we are aware of, so are inner closeness or distance, warmth or coolness, lightness and darkness, fluidity or solidity etc. more fundamentally real than their physical counterparts.

When we speak of someone as 'warm' or see a bright radiance of their gaze, we are not speaking of any physical heat or light emanated by their bodies or eyes. Nor are we 'merely' using terms such as 'warmth' or 'brightness' metaphorically. To believe so is to imply that the warmth or light we feel emanating from a human being is somehow *less real* than a measurable temperature of the human body or the measurable light impinging on or reflected by their eyes.

To speak as many alternative health practitioners do - of such manifest qualities of awareness of soul as 'energies' and to approach a patient's symptoms through one or other variety of so-called 'energy medicine' is to impose a quasi- or pseudo-scientific framework on the most basic elements and qualities of our nature as human beings. At the same time however, it is an evasion of the basic question of what is more real or fundamental – the human body or the human being, energetic relationships betweens bodies in space and time, or inner relationships between beings. To say that it is 'energy' that links or relates things and beings is one thing. But put the other way round, we can equally well say that the essence of energy is *relationality* as such. It is not energy that is the medium of vital interaction between people, but rather active and vital relating that 'energises' or vitalises them.

The principal instrument of organismic healing is the therapist's own felt body – their own subjective organism and organismic awareness. The therapist is someone who has transformed their own undifferentiated 'organismic awareness', 'soma-sensitivity' or 'felt sense' into a new organ of inner cognition - a 'sixth sense'. With this sense they can obtain a direct feeling awareness of the patterned tonalities, qualities and textures *of* awareness that constitute another person's subjective organism or 'body of awareness'. The medium of this direct feeling cognition or awareness of another person's organism is 'feeling tone'. For again, like audible vocal or musical tones, feeling tones combine qualities of warmth and coolness, lightness and darkness, levity and gravity etc just as they also possess different tonal 'colours', different 'timbres', different elemental textures such as fluidity and solidity, airiness or fieriness and different sonic 'shapes' such as roundedness or angularity.

When we say of someone that they are 'warm and friendly', 'cold and hostile', 'remote and arrogant', 'heavy with remorse' etc. we use phrases which, as verbal signifiers, refer to someone's mental-emotional bearing. Let us say that someone with an emotional history of abandonment, abuse or deprivation of human warmth develops a 'cold' outer bearing, perceived perhaps as emotionally defensive, remote, cut off, arrogant or even hostile and aggressive. To describe someone as 'cold' can have such emotional connotations. Yet this shows that in language, as in life, people have not yet developed the capacity to distinguish sensual qualities of organismic *feeling tone* such as inner warmth and coldness, light and darkness etc. from the way these qualities are emotionally experienced and expressed – both in others and in ourselves. But it is precisely the capacity to distinguish the mental-emotional significance and felt organismic sense of particular somatic or behavioural symptoms that is central to soma-semiotics and organismic healing.

The mother's womb does not just feel physically warm and fluid from within but is a place of felt security and warmth of feeling. When we leave our mother's womb however, we continue to dwell in the womb of our own organism, what Winnicott called "somatic indwelling". And within the womb of our organism it is the self – our felt sense of identity - that continues to grow and differentiate through our experiencing of others and otherness in our life world - which constantly seeds, inseminates and fertilises new aspects of self which gestate within us and seek growth, birth and embodiment. When we feel ill, it is not just that we *feel* ill, but that *we* feel ill. Dis-ease, understood as an organismic field state, is also a *self state*. It is comparable to a state of organismic gestation and pregnancy - one which potentially allows us to give birth to new aspects of self.

Pregnancy is not an illness, even though it may be accompanied by symptoms of a different sort or lead to a painful labour with greater or lesser risk of 'complications'. Pregnancy can lead to birth. Like illness it can even result in death – whether of the mother or child. If illness is itself essentially a state of pregnancy however, then conventional medical treatments constitute a form of premature termination or abortion which literally throws out the unborn 'baby' with the bathwater – seeking to eliminate all bodily or behavioural expressions of the self with which we are pregnant. Alternatively medications may be used to diminish the patient's feelings of malaise, their sense of 'carrying' or having to 'bear' something, and the labour pains accompanying the gestation and birth of this self.

Organismic healing on the other hand is founded on a practice of allowing ourselves to feel the symptoms, suffering or pain of dis-ease *more* intensely rather than less, and in this way come to a felt sense of the as-yet unborn self they express. As in the 'Process Oriented Psychology' of Arnold Mindell, it can take the form of actively encouraging the patient to amplify or 'aggravate' their felt sensations of pain or discomfort. What Mindell found was that this could bring about the release of emotions, mental images and inner comprehensions that expressed the felt meaning of their symptoms. Mindell has applied this method to all types of symptoms, and to all dimensions of the patient's experience of illness – mental, emotional and somatic. If a patient fears death for example, he might ask them, there and then, to die – to actually die or feel themselves dying. He understood that for some patients, death itself might be a natural part of their 'process' of healing – of becoming more whole in a way impossible in their physical life and existence. His work, like soma-semiotics and the practice of what I call organismic healing, is therefore a fundamental challenge to the historic and hitherto unquestioned premise of all forms of medicine – the fundamental belief that its purpose is to 'cure' disease and thereby also to prolong *physical* life and the *physical self*. The motto of this work could be simply that 'feeling is healing'. For by fully feeling and following a symptom of disease back to its source in a sensed dis-ease, and allowing the process of that dis-ease to take its course and like the course of a pregnancy, the result will be the gestation and birth of a new bodily sense of *self* and with it, a new *inner bearing* towards the world and other people.

Case Example 3

"A patient with whom I was working was dying of stomach cancer. He was lying in the hospital bed, groaning and moaning in pain. Have you ever seen someone who is dying? It was really quite sad and terrifying. They flip quickly between trance states, ordinary consciousness and extreme pain. Once, when he was able to speak, he told me that the tumour in his stomach was unbearably painful. I had had an idea that we should focus on his proprioception, that is, his experience of the pain, so I told him that since he'd already been operated on unsuccessfully, we might try something new. He agreed, and so I suggested that try to make the pain even worse.

He said he knew exactly how he could do that and told me that the pain felt like something in his stomach trying to break out. If he helped it break out, he said, the pain worsened. He lay on his back and started to increase the pressure in his stomach. He pushed his stomach out and kept pushing and pressing and exaggerating the pain until he felt as if he were going to explode. Suddenly, at the height of his pain, he said 'Oh, Arny, I just want to explode!'. At that point he switched out of his body experience and began to talk to me. He told me that he needed to explode and asked if I would help him to do so. 'My problem', he said 'is that

I've never expressed myself sufficiently, and even when I do it's never enough.'

This problem is an ordinary, psychological problem that appears in many cases, but with him it became somatised and was pressing him now, urgently expressing itself in the form of a tumour. That was the end of our physical work together. He lay back and felt much better. Though he had been given only a short time to live and had been on the verge of death, his condition improved and he was discharged from the hospital. I went to see him afterwards very often, and every time he 'exploded' with me. He'd make noises, shout and scream, with absolutely no encouragement on my part.

... It was then also that I discovered the vital link between dreams and body symptoms. Shortly before he had entered the hospital, the patient dreamed that he an incurable disease and that the medicine for it was like a bomb. When I asked him about the bomb he made a very emotional sound and cried like bomb dropping in the air, 'it goes up in the air and spins around sshhhss ... pfftfff.' At that moment I knew that the cancer was the bomb in his dream ... his body was literally exploding with pent-up expression. In this way his pain became his own medicine ...

In a flash I discovered that there must be something like a dreambody, an entity which is both dream and body at once ... The

SENSING THE PATIENT'S FELT DIS-EASE

way I discovered the concept of the dreambody was through what I called amplification. I amplified my client's body, or proprioceptive experience and I amplified the exploding process which was mirrored in his dream."

Working with the Dreaming Body, Arnold Mindell

Mindell speaks of what I term the 'subjective body', 'organism' or 'felt body' as the 'dreambody'. This is a significant and useful additional term. For it reflects a deep comprehension that symptoms of illness emerge in the same way as *dreams* do and that illnesses can be understood as 'body dreams' – as embodied dreams or nightmares. From this point of view it makes no more sense to regard sickness as an 'unnatural' deviation from a 'normal' state of health than it does to regard dreaming as an unnatural or abnormal disruption of sleep, or to regard nightmares in particular as an 'unhealthy type' of dream. The biomedical model of illness on the other hand, based as it is on the premise that illness is a *meaningless* deviation from health, is as outdated as certain pre-Freudian 'scientific' beliefs that dreams are *meaningless* discharges of neurological energy.

Soma-semiotics understands dreaming as one of two principal functions of the human organism. The other function is *bodying* – the organism being the instrument with which we body forth our capacities of being and give bodily expression to feelings – to inner field states, field qualities and field patterns of awareness. Bodying however, is not the same thing as 'somatising' – the unconscious production of somatic symptoms as an indirect expression and communication of psychological states. On the contrary, 'somatisation' through illness can be understood as the expression of an *incapacity* to 'body' a felt dis-ease – to consciously express and communicate it through the language of the body. In contemporary psychoanalytic models of somatic disorders, somatisation is understood as a failure of symbolisation resulting from *alexithymia* – a deficient lexicon of verbal symbols by which to identify and express feelings of the sort now labelled 'emotional illiteracy'. Psychoanalysis focuses only on the relative poverty or richness of a patient's emotional language or 'literacy' however, whilst ignoring the expressive range, poverty or richness of their body language. This is a serious deficit to psychoanalysis and psychoanalytic therapy. For there are many people with a rich and refined emotional as well as intellectual vocabulary - yet whose vocabulary of expressive body language, facial expressions, looks and gestures is limited in the extreme, thus offering them *no possibility* of expressively bodying and communicating sensed states of dis-ease directly - rather than somatising them in the form of disease symptoms.

Eugene Gendlin's 'Focusing' methods emphasise the importance of 'resonating' back and forth between a felt, bodily sense of dis-ease and its reflection in signifiers such as words and mental images – doing so until the latter feel in full resonance or 'congruence' with the former. And yet only if a patient's verbal *and* non-verbal signifiers, words *and* body language, are 'isomorphic' with felt, bodily sense can they lead to state of 'morphic resonance' (Sheldrake) with the latter and to the 'felt shift' in the individual's sense of self and well-being that Gendlin speaks of.

Diagram 5 represents the process of bodying as a healing process by which the patient, rather than (a) concentrating on the symptoms represented by the black square, is able to (b) find a form of expressive outer body language isomorphic with the shape of their felt dis-ease (represented by the shaded area) and thus (c) overcome the sense of dis-ease as felt from within.

Diagram 5

(a) (b) (c)

As well as referring to 'organ speech', Freud also suggested that speech as such may originally have not served a signifying linguistic function but instead may simply have complemented facial expressions as a form of expressive body language. The new methods of 'organismic healing' concentrate on using a variety of exercises evolved over several decades to teach both therapists and patients to expand the expressive range and intensity of their facial expressions and the look in their eyes. Therapists wishing to practice organismic healing are taught to both read and mirror with their own face and eyes everything they can see in another person's face and eyes. In this way they can come to directly *sense* - with and within their own felt body as a whole - all the expressions of dis-ease, however subtle, that they *see* in the face and eyes of the other. The art of deep face and eye 'reading', together with the art of most precisely 'mirroring' a person's facial expression or a particular look in their eyes, can then allow the therapist to do three important things (a) to literally mirror back to the patient the look and 'face' of their dis-ease, and (b) to do so in such a way that the patient not only feels fully 'seen' but also fully *felt* – sensing as they do the therapist's felt *bodily* resonance with their dis-ease. It also allows the therapist to engage in what I term 'transformative resonance', or 'metamorphic resonance'. By this I mean the capacity to pick up on the glimpse or gleam of a disturbing or 'negative' emotion in the patient's face and eyes and to mirror it back in a way that not only amplifies but positively affirms that emotion – not as a labelled emotion but as a pure wordless quality of *feeling tone* that, like a musical tone, chord or phrase which, however seemingly dark, disturbed or dissonant it may sound, is wholly *valid* – and at the same time irreducible to an emotional *label-word* such as 'anger' or 'rage' which is then seen as 'negative'. For the language of the face and eyes, like the language of music, is *infinitely richer and more refined* than the vocabulary of verbally-named *emotions* in giving bodily expression to what is indeed an infinite range of potential qualities, combinations and intensities of *feeling tones*. Thus what a patient learns to feel in their body – with the aid of the therapist's facial mirroring, as a powerful intensity of 'anger' or 'rage' of which they were previously unaware, may be consciously mirrored back to the patient by the therapist in a *transformed* way - not *as* 'anger' or 'rage' but, for example, as an intensive, emotionally neutral sense of intense strength or power *as such*. By this I do not mean power *over* oneself or others, but the innate power *of* the patient's own being – one that the latter can learn to *fully feel, affirm and embody* through its *total affirmation and expression* in the face and eyes of a therapist capable of sensing and embodying it. I use this particular example of transformative resonance deliberately, for a central characteristic of illness in general is a sense of *powerlessness* - one that is reinforced by a socially conditioned *dependency* on medical practitioners and institutions, and in many cases also by a dependency on pharmaceutical medications as such.

The human organism can be seen, adapting Sheldrake's terms, as a 'morphic body' or *formative* body – the instrument or *organon* with which we *give form* to inner feeling tones, embodying them in muscle and nerve tone, expressing them in the tone of our voice and in the resonance of our words. The human organism is also the embodied *self* – the instrument with which we *personify* our inner being, letting it 'sound through' (*per-sonare*) our facial mask or *persona*. Just as a letter is the silent face of a sound, so is the human face a silent manifestation of inner sounds – organismic feeling tones. The physical body as a whole is the outer *face* of the human organism. But what is manifest in the face and body of the other is *revealed* directly through their eyes. Every tone and coloration of our *gaze* corresponds to a distinct mode of organismic self-experience: a distinct self state or 'I' revealed through our eyes, a distinct way of looking out at the world or into oneself, and a distinct inner bearing or comportment *towards* our own being and other beings; one that may or may not be visible in our physical posture and movements.

In the practice of organismic healing, the stages of the communicative healing cycle are enacted in two modes; firstly through the medium of therapeutic listening and verbal dialogue, and secondly, through silent periods of close-up, face-to-face eye-contact between healer and patient lasting anything from five or ten minutes to an hour or more. In listening mode too however, the therapist listens *with their whole body* and in such a way as to attune their own listening to the patient's organism or felt body as a whole. A basic rule here is that the therapist's verbal responses must never *precede* or *replace* their own silently felt organismic sense of the patient. Nor should they merely signify and communicate this felt sense to the patient in words in the course of a dialogue. Instead the therapist's speech should convey it to the client *dia-logically* - 'through the word' rather than *in* words.

In listening to the patient's own words, the therapist should be particularly alert for what Anzieu terms "formal signifiers". These are key words or phrases used by the patient that signify their own subjective experience of *dis-ease* using metaphors of static or dynamic *form*, whether two-dimensional or three-dimensional. Examples are such expressions as feeling "deflated", "in a whirl", "over-stretched", "going round in circles", "hollow" or "empty inside" *etc*. The therapist as listener needs to understands these metaphors however, as quite *literal* descriptions of sensed organismic states, and may ask the patient to simply feel and show the state in question in their eyes rather than just talking *about* it.

The second mode of organismic healing is one mediated by silent and close-up eye-contact. To begin with the healer may ask the patient – to whatever extent the latter feels able – to allow their eyes to *show* their inner dis-ease or dis-comfort, their mental concerns or troubling emotions. This is where the 'formal signifiers' used by the patient in describing their own felt dis-ease can provide a significant starting point. If the patient has talked about "being in a whirl" for example, they may be asked to feel the whirl in their body as a whole and show it in their eyes. The therapist, who will be sitting face-to-face with the patient, then looks into the patient's eyes, and engages in a process *of organismic mimesis*. By mimicking and mirroring the patient's look the therapist will find themselves gradually able to feel and identify with the organismic state it expresses. In this way they can not only sense but make resonant contact with the patient's organismic state as a self state – mirroring through the look in their own eyes the particular 'I' that looks out through the patient's eyes.

The number of words that can be used to describe the characteristics of a person's look is limitless, embracing not only the entire nomenclature of the emotions (an angry or sad look, fearful or vulnerable look, a resigned, desolate, lonely or despairing look etc.) That is because the look in a person's eyes is capable of revealing a huge range of subtle but distinct *tones* of feeling. This subtlety of expression of the eyes usually far exceeds the person's subtlety of language in describing their own emotional state - which might instead be reduced to common generic terms such as feeling 'depressed', 'stressed' or 'low'. What the eyes reveal ultimately transcends language itself, for each person's looks, however we might label them verbally, are imbued with an irreducibly individual character – revealing unique aspects of the individual human being. Once again it must be stressed that looks do not just express emotional states but *self states* – modes of self-experience. At the same time a person's look reveals their own way of *looking out on* and perceiving the world and other people. When we speak of a glazed or far-away look, an introverted or contemplative look, we are not describing emotions but the direction of their *gaze*, its different foci and loci. If, following Freud, we compare the individual's consciousness to a searchlight, we should not assume through this analogy that it is only the direction or 'focus' of the beam that can be altered - and that its source or *locus* is always a singular subject, self, ego or 'I'. The inner aspects of the human being revealed through their eyes do indeed reveal different foci of consciousness, but each of these foci also has its own specific locus or 'centre' of awareness – revealing where and from what place in themselves – what self – the person is looking out from. They may, for example, be looking out with the eye and 'I' of the vulnerable or hurt child within them, from a more or less rigid ego or from the very depths and spiritual core of their soul. An important exercise I employ with trainees in organismic healing is to get a sense of the nature of the parental figure that the 'child eye' and child 'I' of a person can be seen as looking at or responding to.

Then again, an individual can be more or less up front and *present* in the eyes, or concealed and withdrawn behind them – like a person who approaches a window to look out at the world or retreats from it into the furthest and darkest corner of the room in order to avoid being seen by the friend or stranger peering in. Inner lights may be turned on and off, curtains drawn or shutters or blinds pulled down, like a second, invisible set of eyelids.

Blinking is a principle defence against sustained eye contact with others, as well as a way of not being deeply seen by others and avoiding any sense of deep inner contact with them. The eyes can be used in many ways as defences against really *meeting* another person with one's gaze – whether through blinking or darting from side to side, or through eyes that stare blankly or look away to avoid contact.

Then again, the gaze is a most powerful medium for imparting a wordless message to the other – for example through a look of cold contempt or hatred, an imploring or impatient look, a loving or seductive look, a resentful or respectful look etc. The dimensions that belong to the 'language of the look' are very familiar to somatic psychotherapists, and Alexander Lowen has written specifically of the particular *gaze modes* corresponding to different character-types in the Reichian schema – for example the 'far away look' of the 'schizoid character'.

Case Example 4

In his book *Lifestreams*, David Boadella quotes an account of Reich's work with a patient who suddenly began "seeing the world with new eyes", the fear and hate having gone out of them.

The process began with Reich noticing a new gleam in the patient's eyes, which ...

"....together with the shifting of the eyes and head, had brought up a new expression out of the depths of his eyes and being. It was a flirtatious, come-hither look, a sort of wink, with a raising of the eyelids, eyebrows and forehead and a moving of the eyeballs to one side, accompanied by a suggestive tilting of the head in the same direction. As the therapist began to imitate this expression and the patient began to make better contact with it, the whole face participated in it, at first with a blushing shame-facedness, and then to the tune of a hearty laugh."

Later a 'miracle' happens:

"Suddenly the patient was startled and opened his eyes wide with astonishment. While he was looking at the therapist the latter's face had suddenly become soft, and glowed with light...He saw the world differently, as a good and pleasurable place to be in and as a future place of 'heaven' and not the 'hell' it had been before."

Boadella comments that this breakthrough:

"... was the direct result of the exchange of looks between the two people in the room, a reaching out on the part of the therapist with his own aliveness to contact and excite into activity the

aliveness buried in the person he was dealing with. Without this willingness to read the secret expression and to nurse it into life, any therapeutic encounter is gravely weakened."

"If a person can let his inner self be seen by another, he begins to become recognisable to himself and can then look within, not in the sense of any sterile introspection, but in the sense of learning to love and accept who he is, and so recognise himself."

In the practice of organismic healing it is precisely the practitioner's ability to "read the secret expression" and "nurse it into life" through *mimesis, mirroring* and *modulation* of their own gaze that is central. To do so the healer must first of all be trained to considerably expand the motility of their own facial expressions and looks, learning to both attune and fine-tune the feeling tones communicated through their gaze.

Reich's focus, in the example quoted, was on mirroring a particular expression of vitality in the patient's eyes. The organismic therapist first takes time to see whatever is there to be seen, only then using *mimesis, modulation and messaging* to respond to each and any of the aspects of the patient's being that can be perceived in their look. The therapist may for example, perceive a look of fear in the patient's eyes, and amidst it something like a brief spark of anger or a shadow of sadness.

Through organismic *mimesis* the healer will first of all allow themselves to fully mimic and thereby come to sense and resonate with the feeling tones communicated through the patient's looks – without necessarily having to identify these feeling tones using emotion words such as 'sadness', 'fear' or 'anger'. The healer then begins to *modulate* these feeling tones with their own organism in a way that transforms the way that they are experienced by the patient. In responding to looks of 'sadness', 'fear' or 'anger' for example, the healer may draw on their *own* organismic experience of 'sadness' as a pure organismic sense of 'soul depth', of 'fear' as a pure organismic sensation of 'vitalising excitement, and of 'anger' as a pure organismic sensation of 'vital power' or 'aggressive vitality' - rather than as something *to be feared*. At the same time they might allow the organismic energy of the 'fear' they receive from the patient to enhance and intensify the *vital power* of this 'anger'.

Rather than just mirroring the patient's 'fear' and 'anger' in their eyes then, the healer will use their eyes, face and entire organism to communicate and bear back a *modulated* or *transformed* feeling tone of vital 'excitement' and 'power'. In doing so they will quite consciously *bear back a message* to the patient: the message that "you too can allow yourself to feel your sadness, fear and anger as a natural organismic sense of excitement and aggressive vitality arising from your soul depths, letting yourself feel them fully and show them in your eyes". The message is transmitted wordlessly, *riding* on the silent, resonant communication between healer and patient in the same way that verbal messages ride on resonances of the spoken word.

In organismic healing sessions, sustained periods of silent eye-contact become a medium of deep and direct organismic contact and communication between healer and patient, automatically inducing a state of deep, open-eyed trance. This trance-like state of organismic resonance is comparable to 'harmonic rapport' spoken of by the early Mesmerists. The 'resonant communications' that pass between healer and patient are a rich and profound form of *trance communication*, through which a type of wordless *telepathic* communication becomes possible. That is because feeling tones are not only 'moods' or colourations of feeling, or 'states of being'. They are essentially *wavelengths of feeling awareness and attunement* linking one *being with another* – and thereby also serving as telepathic *carrier waves* through which wordless messages can be borne across from one being *to* another. Through the subtle *modulation* of their own organismic feeling tones in response to the patient, the healer is able to transmit healing messages on the carrier waves of these feeling tones.

The visible communication through face and eyes gives bodily *expression* to this feeling and telepathic communication, something that we would be quite wrong in regarding as a mere illusion generated by 'reading' subtle body signs and signals.

For as John Heron has explained in his article on *The Phenomenology of Social Encounter: the Gaze,* as soon as we turn another person's eyes into a mere *object* of our own gaze to be observed and studied for signs like an ophthalmologist we immediately *cease* to see the light, quality and tone of that person's *gaze.* Conversely, we can only truly 'read' the expression in another person's eyes by seeing the human being and not just their eyes. Similarly, we can only bear across a wordless message to another through our own eyes in a way that truly communicates to and touches them by both modulating our gaze and intending it to communicate a message – not merely by mechanically signalling a particular message. This type of knowingly intended communication and *messaging* though the eyes can be best understood by thinking of what is meant when we speak of giving someone a *knowing look* - a look that *means* a particular human being and no other.

Organismic healing uses sustained, silent and 'resonant' eye-contact as a medium of both diagnosis and healing. In its root Greek sense the word 'diagnosis' means 'through knowing' (*dia-gnosis*). And yet the type of knowing referred to by the Greek word *gnosis* was not knowledge 'of' or 'about' *something*. It was the sort of knowing we refer to when we speak of knowing *someone* i.e. knowing another being and not merely knowing something *about* that being. Within the framework of a soma-semiotic approach to illness, the practices of organismic healing and 'dia-gnosis' described above also need to be preceded and contextualised within (1) a detailed life picture of the larger biographical story and timing of the patient's illness – when and in what life *context* its symptoms first emerged and (2) a detailed medical picture of its bodily *text* – the exact physiological functions and processes involved in it. It was for this reason that, inspired by the 'pathosophical' understanding of illness derived from Viktor von Weizsäcker, the Argentinean psychoanalyst Luis Chiozza developed a new team approach to the study and treatment of the 'organic patient' – bringing physicians and psychotherapists together to piece together what he calls a 'pathobiography' of the patient – the hidden story of their illness.

The pathobiographical method begins with a series of four to five in-depth interviews with the patient through which an 'anamnesis' of their biography is taken. This is complemented by the patient being given three writing assignments (a) a synopsis of a novel (b) a film plot and (c) a short story. In addition the patient is asked to provide photographs that represent significant moments and people in their lives. Together with the results of a medical examination by doctors and specialists, the team of physicians and psychotherapists then together prepare a synopsis both of the patient's life history and medical history and condition. A 'Clinical Athenaeum' is then held in which this synopsis is analysed with the view to preparing a 'pathobiography'. This takes the form of an oral and textual 'resignification' of the patient's life story, but in terms which aim to reveal the symbolic parallels between (1) significant biographical events in the patient's life story (2) metaphorically significant elements of their medical history and the physiology of their illness. The conclusions and therapeutic indications of the pathobiography are then shared with the patient through a series of further meetings.

The pathobiography gathered from and shared with the patient in this way by the clinical team is not only a diagnostic instrument but the main instrument of therapy - its presentation to and discussion with the patient being designed to induce a direct awareness of the significance of their symptoms in the context of their life as a whole. In this way it can open up the patient for the first time to new dimensions of awareness and insight into the larger life context and meaning of their illness, as well as offering the patient an opportunity to evolve and embody a new inner bearing towards their lives - one which transcends the specific circumstances and condition in which their illness first emerged as a somatic signifier or form of 'organ speech'.

Case Example 5

In his book *Hidden Affects in Somatic Disorders* Chiozza presents a series of 'pathobiographical studies', each of which is designed not only to shed light on the 'hidden story' of a particular patient's illness, but in doing so to reveal the general psychical significance of a particular organ and organic dysfunction. Indeed in each case Chiozza begins by considering organic functions themselves as psychical signifiers, then moves on to analysing the signification of specific organic dysfunctions, and finally links these to significant patterns of events in the individual patient's life.

What follows is a summary of Chiozza's pathobiographical study, not just of a particular psoriatic patient but thereby also of the type of psychical disposition that, according to Chiozza, may in general predispose an individual to developing psoriasis. The starting point of his study is the general psychical signification of the *skin* as container for the self and as contact surface with others. This echoes Freud's view that "the ego is first and foremost a bodily ego", having its source in "bodily sensations, chiefly those springing from the surface of the body". This is the key idea developed in Anzieu's concept of the "ego skin" or "skin ego". For Chiozza on the other hand "the skin exists as an organ simultaneously with the fantasy of a skin-ego" and the latter is not to be considered as something derivative of the former. Psychical and somatic skins are understood as joint expressions of something more fundamental than either. Chiozza seeks this 'thing in itself' or 'skin in itself' through its expression in key linguistic signifiers with a double vector of signification, capable of being used to refer both to a psychical and physical skin.

Examples of skin signifiers:

irritable / inflamed / exposed / vulnerable / wounded / raw
thin-skinned / thick-skinned / sensitive / insensitive
to get under one's skin / to develop a hard skin / second skin
to be flayed by criticism/ to be skinned alive

In order to understand the pathobiography of a particular skin disorder such as psoriasis, Chiozza also attends to the deeper symbolic significance which can be discovered in its pathophysiology. Thus he interprets the *hyperkeratosis* or thickening of the corneal layer of the skin as an attempt by the patient to develop a 'thick skin' as protection against hyper-sensitivity to criticism or rejection, or a lack of 'caressing' praise and comforting contact. Both contact deprivation and flaying criticism or lack of caressing lead to contact avoidance – aided by the shame experienced by the patient at his or her own diseased skin.

Physiologically, however, the hyperkeratosis involves an over-production of immature cells deficient in their ability to produce keratin – this reflecting, in Chiozza's understanding, an accelerated, precocious but incomplete growth of the ego. Their adhesion being defective, corneal cells are constantly shed – flaking, peeling or scaling off. The psoriatic patient's 'thick skin' is the constantly shed surface of a sensitive, inflamed and reddened substrate, accentuated by the proliferation of sub epidermal blood vessels. Chiozza sees the constant desquamation or shedding of scaly skin as analogous to a reptile regularly sloughing off its own scaly skin. He understands this as a physiological metaphor of the constantly failing attempt on the part of the psoriatic patient to replace one skin with another – in order to adapt to their environment and achieve the longed-for sense of acceptance and recognition and supportive social contact. In practice the result is the very opposite, producing a surface appearance that accentuates the patient's self-disgust – a continuing fear of rejection by others that goes together with self-rejection. This self-rejection is reflected physiologically in the fact that psoriasis is also considered a type of auto-immune disorder.

In his accompanying pathobiography of the individual patient he describes, Chiozza attaches particular significance to a number of events and emotions in the patient's life: his feeling of aloneness following a move to another country at the age of fourteen; his felt need to take care of his mother, who became mentally ill after the move; how scared he was by his mother's symptoms; his felt lack of affectionate physical contact from both parents; his fear of and subsequent desertion by his girlfriend; his attempt to harden himself in the face of this desertion and be tough enough to face life alone despite his feelings of hurt and vulnerability; his taking responsibilities in his father's factory but being scathed with criticism and shamed in front of other employees.

Chiozza sees in these events someone who needed to grow up fast and develop a thick skin to take care of his mother, who adopted adult responsibilities only to be met with wounding criticism and who still bore the burden of an unmet need to be taken care of, caressed and comforted himself – against which he still attempted to toughen himself up. As is often the case in psychoanalytic case descriptions however, the "hidden affects" or "unconscious fantasies" which Chiozza sees as so important in understanding illness seem in this case, as in others, not to be a 'hidden story' or 'unconscious' at all, but rather to have been affects consciously experienced by the patient in the course of his life.

Chiozza's allusion to a more fundamental reality behind both somatic symptoms and the verbal signifiers associated with them, confirms the soma-semiotic understanding that the human organism can itself be identified neither with the physical body or brain nor with the mind or psyche – or a mental body of linguistic signifiers. Instead it is itself a psychical *body* or 'body of awareness'. The thick skin sought by the psoriatic patient is neither a physical skin nor a mental skin. The patient's precociously and precariously hardened mental and physical skin both stood in, as signifiers, for a secure organismic skin. This organismic skin does indeed have a reality more fundamental than either the fleshly skin or mental 'ego skin'. For whilst the ego may indeed be thought of as a mental image or projection of the physical body's skin surface or boundary, the organismic skin is a more or less porous or rigid boundary between the field of our outer sensory awareness of the world around us, and the boundless inner field of awareness of the sort long associated with the 'soul'.

Whether we speak of 'handling' someone with care, of their being irritably 'thin-skinned' or impenetrably 'thick skinned', it is essentially neither the physical skin we are referring to nor a way of touching them, but rather our handling of their soul *as a* body in its own right – the organism as a 'subjective body' or 'body of awareness'. What is missing in Chiozza's analysis is an understanding of his patient's lack of inner soul contact with others – not through a lack of appropriate verbal or physical handling alone but through a lack of sensitivity in handling his soul.

What Chiozza also ignores is the crucial *respiratory* function of the skin, a symbol of the individual's capacity to fully 'take in' - breathe in and absorb - their awareness of the spacious, air- and light-filled world around them, and to do so through their body surface as a whole and not just through localised sense organs on or near that surface.

As is typical in psychotherapeutic discourse, Chiozza's key analytical signifiers are almost entirely affectual – referring to emotions of fear, loss, isolation, shame, humiliation, woundedness, vulnerability, rage, disgust etc. By definition however, an 'emotion' is an e-motion – an outward motion of awareness from the individual's organismic core to its surface periphery or skin. Understood symbolically, skin disorders in particular are an expression not of 'deeply buried' or 'unconscious' affects but of emotions 'just below the surface'. Organismic healing, for a patient such as that described by Chiozza, would consist in truly getting beneath the skin of these surface emotions and their somatic expression, and providing genuine inner support and 'holding' – giving the patient the supportive psychical containment and contact that he lacked in the past. For in the history of the psoriatic patient, as Chiozza points out, it is not a lack of skin contact or affirmative verbal communication that counts but the sense of psychical containment that these can provide – for example through the enveloping and contactful embrace of the parent or the enveloping world of fantasy images provided by parental storytelling. The other side of the story however is the one I have already alluded to – the role of the skin as a sense organ and respiratory organ for the body as a whole, one that can either seal us off from or porously open us and allow us to 'breathe in' the spacious field of sensory awareness and experiencing that constitutes our outer world.

In Chiozza's analysis of the 'psoriatic character', as in his analyses of the 'diabetic' or 'asthmatic' character, he is at pains to point out that he is referring to a psychical *disposition* only. It does not mean that the individual will necessarily contract the disease associated with this disposition. Nevertheless, should they do so, this is a clear sign of such a disposition. The latter however, cannot be identified with a purely psychological' (mental-emotional) disposition. Nor is it reducible to a genetic disposition. Instead it needs to be seen both as an *organismic* and as an *existential* disposition – as an embodied inner bearing toward their life story and life world which may be more or less restrictive and find expression in a more or less rigid posture or body language. The purpose of illness as a state of pregnancy is precisely to initiate a process by which, through awareness of its meaning, the individual can learn through their own body to give birth to and *embody* a new inner bearing toward the world and other people – for example through a new capacity to 'feel at home' in their own skin, to make it more naturally open and porous to breathing in their sensory awareness of the world, or relax an otherwise cramped musculature and/or mode of vocal and bodily communication with others.

Mental patterns of thought and emotional experiencing are not something separate from the human organism as a whole but are a part of it – a skin or skein of thoughts constituting its periphery and the 'emotions' reflecting *motions of awareness* both to and from that periphery (both e-motions and 'in-motions'). Like any skin or membrane the organismic periphery has an inner and an outer surface that are both distinct and inseparable. The outer surface is a patterned web or nexus of significance constituted by thought and language, mental and verbal signifiers. This can be considered, as Freud intuited, as a "projection" of sensations arsing primarily from the body's surface. But our inner feeling awareness of these same sensations has at the same time an immediately felt sense or meaning. Similarly, our own thoughts in the form of mental words and speech have inner resonances or undertones with their own depths of wordlessly sensed meaning.

The peripheral 'skin' of the organism can thus be visualised - like our bodily skin - as having three distinct layers (ectoderm, mesoderm and endoderm).

The Threefold Layering of the Organismic Periphery:

1. Ectoderm – and outer mind skin or 'ego skin' consisting of verbal signifiers.

2. Mesoderm - an emotional skin or 'self skin' consisting of surface physical sensations, including skin sensations themselves.

3. Endoderm – a 'soul skin' that is the inner surface of a boundless inner space of wordlessly felt meaning or sense.

The first layer can be compared to text or images printed on a sheet of paper, the second layer to the sheet of paper itself – manifest as our fleshly skin. The third layer is the medium for a proprioceptive awareness of the invisible but boundless interiority or 'space' of meaning or sense within the text.

The 'ego skin' corresponds to what Winnicott called the 'mind psyche'. The emotional or self-skin is the boundary of what he called the 'psyche-soma'. This is indeed the skin that we refer to when we describe someone as sensitive, irritable or 'thick-skinned'. But that skin has an underside and inside – being the inner surface of an unbounded psychic interiority of awareness consisting of felt sensual qualities and textures of awareness. As these rise from within to the surface and permeate the self-skin and ego-skin they become emotions and thoughts. Yet not all emotions are essentially e-motions or outward motions arising from within. Sadness and depression are essentially inward motions or 'in-motions' of awareness from the individual's ego-skin or self-skin to the deeper interiority or 'soul space' of the psyche within.

"You will not find the limits of the soul by going around (its surface) even through you go in every direction, so deep is its inner speech." Heraclitus

In semiotic terms, the organismic 'skin', surface or periphery can be considered as a *semiosphere* of signifiers or signified senses surrounding and concealing an *unbounded* inner space of awareness or *noosphere* – the realm of sensed significance belonging to the individual's inner bodily self-awareness. It is when the space of this inner bodily self-awareness contracts that symptoms manifest on the organismic periphery – not just as skin symptoms but as somatic symptoms of any sort.

When inner awareness is withdrawn from a part of our body we feel it not as a part of our own embodied self or inner "I" but as a foreign body or "It". The more localised the area from which awareness is withdrawn the more it is experienced as *pain* – pain being a sensation which most forcibly *directs* and *calls back* awareness to a specific region of our body.

A central principle of organismic healing is that the less aware we are of our *inwardly sensed body and of our sensory world as a whole* the less aware we are of our *being or self as a whole*. Unfortunately however, we live in a culture in which, despite being characterised by an overload of sensory stimuli – for example through the visual media - and an obsession with sexual stimulation, bodily self-awareness or 'proprioception' remains a highly undeveloped sense – one that is usually only awakened either through localised sensations of pleasure or pain, or when our bodies as a whole feel pervaded by a sense or mood of dis-ease. The central practice of organismic healing, both in relation to 'physical' and 'mental' illness can therefore be summed up in a single phrase – 'coming to our senses'. This in turn however, is impossible without a proprioceptive awareness of our body as a whole – and in particular our own skin, for the skin is not just a respiratory organ but our most primordial organ not just of tactile sensing but of *sensory awareness* as such – allowing us to breathe in our awareness of the entire sensory world around us, and to be aware of the entire space surrounding our bodies in all directions. Without a proprioceptive awareness of our own body surface as a whole, we can neither use it to sense and take in the entire space surrounding our bodies, nor sense the unbounded inner space or deep interiority of soul that our felt body surface or skin itself surrounds and bounds. Nor can we experience any form of respiratory inhalation or exhalation of our sensory experiencing of the world of the sort suggested by another of the sayings of Heraclitus: "The soul is an exhalation that perceives."

The reason that people go for walks to refresh and revitalise themselves is that they no sooner leave their houses than their proprioceptive sense of their own skin surface is awakened by sensations of space, of air temperature or breezes, or of light. Similarly, the reason that, coming across and viewing the broad or deep expanse of a flat or mountainous landscape, people find themselves spontaneously taking a deep breath, is that in doing so they have a felt sense of taking or breathing in an expanded awareness of space – an awareness that reaches to the very horizon of their vision or hearing and is therefore no longer felt bounded by their own heads or bodies. They are no longer merely looking out at the spacious world around them as if through the 'peepholes' of the senses, but sensing the spaciousness of that world with and from their body surface as a whole.

The field of our outer sensory awareness of the world has multiple dimensions – visual, auditory etc. all of which also have a *tactile* feeling dimension, allowing us not just to see but to feel – even at a distance - the rippling waves on an ocean, the texture and densities of rock and tree, the spatial heights of the sky or a mountain, the depths of a valley, or the verdant expanse of a forest. The same *tactile intensity* of outer sensory experiencing can be enjoyed not just in nature but also in towns and cities, indeed in the seemingly confined spaces of our own homes. All we need do is to cease merely seeing 'as' – for example, not longer seeing something 'as' a car, street lamp, rubbish bin or brick building façade, but simply taking in whatever we see in as we would a so-called 'abstract' sculpture, painting or installation, i.e. as nothing abstract at all but rather as something concrete - as a *purely sensual* shape or form. To see a red road sign, shop front, car or flower simply as a red road sign, shop front, car, brick wall or flower – *that* is a wholly 'abstract', *desensualised* mode of perception. On the other hand, to attend to, appreciate and take in the purely sculptural, textural and chromatic qualities of a sensory phenomenon – that is truly 'concrete' and tangible sensory experiencing, enabling us to experience the sensory qualities of a thing *with and within* our own body as a whole and not just through the peepholes of the senses. Doing so will make us aware of all the sensory qualities of things as manifestations of innately sensual qualities *of awareness as such*, of the sort that make up the sensed inner spaces of our own bodies. In this way the 'outer senses' belonging to our bodies become expressions of inner senses and sensual qualities belonging to our inner awareness of our bodies themselves.

These include:

1. Our felt sense of the openness or closedness, breathing porosity of our body surface as a whole.

2. Our felt sense of the qualitative expanse or restricted bodily enclosure of our awareness.

3. Our felt sense of the lightness and darkness, brilliance or dullness of our awareness and its different mood colourations.

4. Our felt sense of the groundedness, centeredness, balance and stability of our awareness.

5. Our felt sense of the density and substantiality of our awareness as such – its solidity, fluidity or airiness.

6. Our felt sense of the inner warmth or coolness of feeling that permeates our awareness of things and people.

7. Our felt sense of inner closeness to or distance from other people.

8. Our felt inner sense of touching or contacting something or someone in our awareness.

9. Our felt inner sense of the rest and motion, acceleration and deceleration of our awareness.

10. Our felt inner sense of different inner and outer directions of motion of awareness - of emotions themselves as both moods and motions of awareness.

Together, these senses constitute the felt meaning or 'sense' of our sensory experiencing of the world. They are also what inform our bodily sense of self, of others and of other selves latent within us. At the basis of all ten inner senses is our most fundamental 'inner sense'. This is our inner sense of different moods or *tonalities* of awareness or 'feeling tones'. From this *primary* inner sense arises also our most *pervasive* inner sense – our sense of inner harmony or resonance or inner dissonance and dis-ease. Together with the ten senses listed above, therefore, we can add three more.

11. Our inner sense of meaning and intent.

12. Our inner sense of self and others.

13. Our inner sense of resonance and dissonance.

The inner senses are not only expressed in sensory and aesthetic experience but also embodied in organic functions of the physical body. We can also speak of three primary 'organismic' senses which have specifically to do with 'organic' functions.

14. Our sense of *inner respiration* – the inhalation and exhalation of different qualities of awareness through our subjective organism or body of awareness.

15. Our sense of *inner circulation* – of the qualitative flows of awareness we sense within our organism or body of awareness.

16. Our sense of *inner metabolism* – of the process of digesting and metabolising our experiencing of ourselves, other people and our life world as a whole.

The less consciously or effectively we exercise these inner organismic capacities the more likely they are to express themselves as disturbances of organic functions.

From a soma-semiotic perspective there are eight basic dynamics governing the *relation* between organismic capacities such as the respiration, circulation and metabolism of experience, and, on the other hand the organic functions through which these capacities are embodied.

1. A weakened organismic capacity weakens a bodily function.

2. A weakened organic function weakens an organismic capacity.

3. A strengthened organismic capacity strengthens an organic function.

4. A strengthened organic function strengthens an organismic capacity.

5. An organic function compensates for an under-active organismic capacity.

6. An over-active organic function weakens an organismic capacity.

7. A weakened organismic capacity strengthens an organic function.

8. A weakened organic function strengthens an organismic capacity.

Thus for example, an over-strong organismic immune system – in essence an over-rigid boundary between 'self' and 'other' or 'self' and 'world', may be compensated for by a weakening of the body's organic immune system – making it more prone to infection by so-called 'non-self' pathogens such as bacteria, viruses, even though these are always permanently present in huge numbers in a 'healthy' body.

In his major work entitled "The Organism" the neurologist Kurt Goldstein described how organismic capacities are exercised in the form of ordered or organised performances such as walking or talking, writing or reading, calculating or describing. The latter are in turn a response to a specific social and environmental field or 'milieu'. If organs are damaged these performances are hindered. Not being able to embody certain capacities through the functioning of its organs the organism cannot 'function' properly i.e. cannot respond adequately to a particular milieu. This does not mean however, that it is incapable of coping in a different milieu. Goldstein's point is that organic 'disease', even among animals, is not something intrinsic to a living organism but has to do with the relationship between an organism and its milieu. Every change in this relation alters both. For human beings in particular however, loss of ability to exercise their capacities and fulfil their potentials through ordered performances in their existing milieu can be experienced as a "catastrophic" threat – a loss of meaning and of being or "essence". The threat is felt as catastrophic because, for Goldstein:

"...the organism's being is its raison d'être. All individual processes take their meaning from and are determined by this being. We describe this as the organism's essence."

As a result, health:

"... is not an objective condition which can be understood by the methods of natural science alone. It is rather a condition related to the mental attitude by which the individual has to value what is essential for his life. 'Health' appears thus as a value; its value consists in the individual's capacity to actualise his nature to the degree, that for him at least, is essential. 'Being sick' appears as a loss or diminution of value, the value of self-realisation, of existence."

Health, in other words, is not the physical or mental ability of an individual to function effectively or 'normally' within a pre-given physical or social environment – their milieu. Health is value fulfilment – the individual's ability to find or shape a milieu in which their intrinsic values or potentials of being can be fulfilled as capacities through ordered performances.

According to Goldstein, every organism, including the human organism, dwells in two environments – a 'positive' one to which it can respond effectively through its performances and a 'negative' one to which it cannot. Together these make up its milieu. Disease is not the expression of an inborn genetic 'weakness' of the organism in 'adapting' to its environment, but an inability on the part of the individual being to adapt that environment to its needs – to find or create the appropriate milieu for itself. Stimuli impinging from a negative environment may damage organs, disturb, derange or disable the organism's responses and performances or render them inadequate. The natural response of the individual is to avoid such impingements and/or to alter its environment and restrict its particular milieu so that it places less demands on functions that are organically impaired – or in danger of becoming so.

Neither the bodily nor the behavioural symptoms of 'disease' therefore, necessarily point to organic 'causes'. Instead they may themselves be healthy and adaptive organismic responses to a negative environment – an attempt to escape that environment or transform it into a less demanding or more life-enhancing milieu.

Finally, we must remember that the individual too, is on one level a cell within the living environment of a larger social body or organism that may itself be more or less healthy. The health of the individual cannot be privatised - separated from the general health of human relations in society – the health of the social organism.

That is why Maslow rejected "our present easy distinction between sickness and health, at least as far as surface symptoms are concerned".

"Does sickness mean having symptoms? I maintain now that sickness might consist of not having symptoms when you should. Does health mean being symptom-free? I deny it. Which of the Nazis at Auschwitz or Dachau were healthy? Those with a stricken conscience or those with a nice, clear, happy conscience? Was it possible for a profoundly human person not to feel conflict, suffering, depression, rage, etc.?"

A sick social organism may reject a healthy cell, treating an individual – or an entire group – as a malignant foreign body or pathogen. If the individual suffers or even becomes sick as a result of this, is this a healthy response or not?

Is it the task of medical science and practice to seek the technological annihilation or 'final solution' to all symptoms of social dis-ease or of the individual's dis-ease with society? Or is its fundamental task to tackle sickness of the social organism itself, a sickness of human relations that lie at the heart of both individual and social ill-health, and one that is no more clearly expressed than in its own *pathological* forms of medical diagnosis and treatment?

Organismic healing is 'medicine beyond medicine' or 'meta-medicine' - a way of transcending all forms of medicine which objectify the human body and reduce the individual's subjectively felt *dis-ease* into a mere 'case' of some generic 'disease' - rather seeing it as an expression of their life dilemmas and distress, and of their life story and life world as a whole. It is *life medicine* and *life doctoring* of a sort that makes use of the physician's own body as a principle instrument or *organon* for directly sensing and resonantly transforming the patient's felt dis-ease, and through it, their sense of self and relation to their life world.

Summary

...somatic resonance in medicine and mental health

Psychiatric services concentrate primarily on the symptomology, neurophysiology, and pharmacotherapy of mental illness. Counselling and psychotherapy offer 'talking therapies' focused on the client's mental-emotional states. Social work concerns itself with the provision of managed social care for the mentally ill. Approaches to 'mental illness' which concentrate either on mental-emotional states or on brain chemistry, however, tend both to encourage a lack of sensitivity to the *somatic* dimensions of the client's experience of mental illness - their *bodily sense* of dis-ease or distress and their felt bodily sense of *self* – or lack of it. And yet deepening a client's their *bodily* sense of self and of inner connectedness to others should be regarded as a central aim of therapy. Unfortunately however, both psychopharmacology and counselling or psychotherapy can also have the very opposite effect. Pharmacotherapeutic treatment may numb rather than deepen the client's bodily sense of self and of inner connectedness to others. And 'talking cures' of all forms can become a substitute for deep *somatic* sensitivity and resonance on the part of the therapist.

When either the physically ill or the mentally disturbed 'ill' turn to health professionals for help they are not just seeking medical diagnosis and treatment – nor even are they merely seeking 'emotional' empathy and support. They are looking for someone capable of fully receiving them as *some-body* - and not just as a talking head. By this I mean someone sensitive enough to resonate with those felt bodily dimensions of their lived experience that are so difficult to communicate in words. Not finding professionals with sufficient *soma-sensitivity* to 'resonate' with an individual's inwardly sensed body, the client may feel no choice but to continue to communicate their felt dis-ease, suffering or 'pathos' through some form of bodily or behavioural, somatic or social 'pathology'.

The theoretical framework of *soma-semiotics* offers a *relational* model of psychopathology. The 'primary relation' addressed however, is the individual's relation to their own felt body and bodily sense of self. Different recognised medical diseases or psychiatric disorders are understood not as physical, mental or emotional disorders, but as *distortions* in the individual's *relation* to their own felt bodies and to their bodily sense of themselves, other people and the world around them.

In many current forms of medical and mental health treatment the *meaning* of a client's pathology is sought in a hypothetical 'cause' or represented in the concepts, categories and constructs of a specific theoretical model. In contrast, soma-semiotics follows the work of Eugene Gendlin in acknowledging that meaning or *sense* is something that can be directly felt and *sensed* in a bodily way – and that a physician or therapist's own felt bodily sense of a client – their 'soma-sensitivity' - can provide a deeper foundation for a truly therapeutic response than any pre-established 'body' of medical or psychological concepts, diagnostic categories or therapeutic techniques.

Gendlin's own groundbreaking work on the importance of bodily sensing in psychotherapy arose from research into the distinguishing characteristics of those clients who - independently of the nature of their own presenting problem and the particular approach of the practitioner – seemed able to benefit from therapy more than others. His conclusion was that such clients were naturally able to use bodily sensing to (a) *feel for* words with which to express otherwise murky or unclear aspects of their experience, and (b) *check out* whether their own or other people's verbal articulation of a problem was in resonance with their direct somatic experience of it. From this insight arose a new basic principle of therapeutic *practice*, a principle which provided at the same time an important new way of *evaluating* the efficacy of therapeutic interventions *in situ*.

"Moment by moment, after anything a person says or does, one must attend to the effect it has on what is directly experienced. Does a given statement, interpretation, cognitive restructuring or any symbolic expression bring a step of change in how the problem is concretely, somatically experienced? ... If there was no effect, we can discard what was said or done."

In these words of Gendlin we find implicit *the* central distinction that lies at the basis of soma-semiotics, i.e. between a realm of *signified sense* ("...a given statement, interpretation, cognitive restructuring or any symbolic expression" on the one hand and that of *sensed significance* ("...how the problem is concretely, somatically experienced").

'Focusing' is the name Gendlin gave to a set of simple but highly effective methods which could help precisely those clients who had *difficulty* benefiting from therapy. The techniques of Focusing concentrate on helping the client – or any individual – to feel their feelings in a direct bodily way. This in turn enables them to sense whether their words or actions are in *resonance* with their own immediate *somatic* sense of their own situation or state of being.

It is not immediately clear from the citation from Gendlin above whether he is referring to an individual's own "...statement, interpretation, cognitive restructuring or any symbolic expression" *and/or* to that of a therapist. Soma-semiotics draws from Gendlin's method of Focusing but shifts *its* focus from exploring the factors which enable *clients* to benefit from therapy, to the factors which enable therapists and counsellors to be successful – irrespective of the particular approach they adopt. Rather than examining and comparing the various models and methods, strategies and skills, processes and procedures which different schools of therapy employ, it concentrates on the dimensions of awareness that make individual therapists successful – in particular their own bodily self-awareness and sensitivity to the body of the client.

The *practical* focus of soma-semiotics therefore, is not just on the bodily self-awareness of the client or patient but on the soma-sensitivity and capacity for somatic resonance of the medical or mental health professional themselves. Its aim is to cultivate the *therapist's* ability to use 'bodily sensing' to (a) check out the efficacy of their own therapeutic interventions, (b) to become more sensitive to somatic dimensions of the client's self-experience, and (c) use their own felt body to *resonate with* and *transform* the client's inner bodily sense of self.

As Gendlin has pointed out, 'therapy' itself is best understood not as some 'thing' that one person is trained to 'give' to another, but as a process – one that can either be facilitated or hindered in *any* relationship, including the 'therapeutic relationship'. The therapeutic value of soma-semiotics comes from its focus on the *relational* significance of 'bodily sensing' and the innately therapeutic benefit of 'soma-sensitivity' to the patient or client.

Training in soma-sensitivity therefore offers a valuable new form of complementary training and continued professional development for all those working as medical or mental health practitioners.

The cultivation and therapeutic practice of soma-sensitivity and somatic resonance is understood in a different way to that of other, neo-Reichian forms of 'somatic' or 'body-oriented' psychotherapy – none of which make any *fundamental* distinction in principle between the physical body on the other and the individual's subjectively felt or sensed body on the other.

"The body is an awareness."

Carlos Castaneda

In most forms of somatic psychotherapy the *felt body* is reduced simply the way we inwardly sense or feel our *physical bodies* – rather than being recognised as an independent body in its own right, not a 'objective' body of molecules, cells and organs within a physical environment but a body of cellular, molecular and organic and environmental *awareness.*

Soma-semiotics transcends the artificial separation of physical and 'mental' illness, somatic medicine and psychotherapy, organic and 'psychosomatic' illness. Physical body functions such as respiration, digestion and metabolism are the expression of basic functions of our felt body as a body of *awareness* body – for example our capacity to inhale, digest and metabolise our *awareness* of the world and other people. Both physical and mental illness are the expression of inner body states.

Physical illness is the expression of disturbed inner-body functions – the respiration, circulation, digestion and metabolism of awareness. So-called 'mental' illness is an expression of a disturbed relation to the inwardly sensed body and self as such. This disturbed relation however, is invariably felt both as a 'mental' state and as a bodily or somatic state. States of anxiety, depression, dissociation or depersonalisation for example are all felt in a bodily way and in this way affect the individual's bodily sense of self. Indeed specific psychiatric disorders such as schizophrenia, depression, bipolar disorder, or borderline personality disorder can all be understood as expressing specific disturbances in the individual's *relation* to their bodily sense of self. What is regarded in the West as the 'disease' of 'depression' for example, (a word with no equivalent in Japanese) can be understood as the expression of a culturally induced incapacity to actively *depress* awareness from the head and upper regions of the inwardly sensed body to the abdomen and lower body. For it is in this way that we *reground* and *recentre* our inner bodily self-awareness, restoring a healthy sense of what Winnicott called "psycho-somatic indwelling". Schizophrenia, on the other hand, is the expression of a split between the inwardly sensed body or *psyche-soma* (Winnicott) and the inner space of our minds or *mind-psyche*.

As Japanese philosopher Sato Tsuji pointed out:

"It is the great error of Western philosophers that they always regard the human body intellectually, from the outside, as though it were not indissolubly a part of the active self."

Viewed from the outside, self and body are both seen as something bounded by our own skins, and separated from others by an empty space filled only by air. But there is a deep reason why the root meaning of the Greek words *psyche* and *pneuma* originally meant 'breath' and 'wind', and why the words 'spirit' and 'respiration' have a common derivation from the Latin *spirare* – to breathe. For in what manner and at what point does the air we breathe in become a part of 'us' and 'our' body? And at what point or in what manner does the air we breathe out cease to be part of 'us' and 'our' body? The question cannot be answered except by suspending our ordinary notion of self and body. Our felt body has no physical or fleshly boundaries but is an *awareness* that, like the air we inhale and exhale, also flows *between* us and the world, and, like air as such pervades the entire space of our outer sensory awareness of the world.

The deep connection between awareness and breathing was well recognised in the spiritual traditions of the East, where meditation meant centring both *awareness and breathing* in the abdomen or *hara* (Japanese) rather than the chest. Individuals in our globalised Western culture, on the other hand, tend feel their breathing as something centred solely in their head and chest, and their very sense of self as located in their head and/or heart alone. Not being *grounded* in lower body awareness – individuals lack a sense of inner *centeredness* in the lower abdomen or *hara* - that abode of the soul which in Japanese culture has always been understood as both the physical and spiritual *centre of gravity* of the human being.

In Greek culture the word *soma* originally referred simply to a lifeless corpse devoid of *psyche* or 'life breath'. Only later did the word *soma* come to refer to the living body of the human being, and the word *psyche* to its sensed interiority or 'soul-space'. Today however, the very term *psychology* has become a contradiction in terms, referring to a 'science' in which soul or *psyche* has no place, or in which it is identified with the mind or brain. Its connection with the individual's inwardly sensed body is completely ignored. Only in the work of Winnicott do we find a recognition that mental health has to do with the *psyche-soma* as opposed to the *mind-psyche* – our capacity to dwell and feel at home not just in the mind-space of our heads but the inner 'soul space' of our bodies, understood as a space of *awareness* that extends outwards to embraces our entire sensory world and every other body within it.

The Nature of the Sensed Body

What *body* is it with which we feel 'warmer' or 'cooler', 'closer' or more 'distant' to someone – independently of our physical temperature and physical distance from them? What *body* are we referring to when we speak of being 'touched' by someone without any physical contact, of moving 'closer' to them or 'distancing' ourselves from them, of feeling 'uplifted' or 'carried away'? Are these phrases merely emotional metaphors derived from motions in physical space, or are the emotions themselves expressions of basic *motions* of awareness belonging to an inner body of awareness – that 'soul body' which Winnicott referred to as the *psyche-soma*, and Jung as the 'subtle body'? What body and what organs are we referring to when we speak of someone being 'warm-hearted' or 'heartless', 'thick-skinned' or 'thin-skinned', 'stable' or 'unstable', 'balanced' or 'imbalanced', 'solid' or 'mercurial', 'stable' or 'volatile'? Are we simply using bodily 'metaphors' to describe disembodied mental or emotional. Or are we describing innate bodily qualities of an individual's awareness as such – somatic qualities of *soul*.

The body as perceived from without is *a sensory image of the soul* – its mark or sign (Greek *semeion*). At the same time the body as sensed from within is a *sense organ of the soul*, facilitating soma-sensitivity and somatic resonance with the inwardly sensed body o another.

Soma-sensitivity and somatic resonance are the capacity to sense and thus come to resonate with another person's mental-emotional states and 'feelings' in a bodily way – as sensed and sensual qualities and *motions* of their own inwardly sensed body. The words or verbal signifiers that serve as expressions of soma-sensitivity to another will thus themselves tend to be purely *sensual* rather than mental or emotional terms. Thus we may come to sense someone as 'fragmented', 'frozen' in panic, 'hollow' or 'empty' inside, 'walled in' or 'closed off', 'volatile' or about to 'burst' etc. Again however. such expression are not 'merely' emotional metaphors but literal descriptions of the felt qualities and states of *awareness* that dominate another person's bodily sense of their own 'state of being'. These *felt states* can be understood as *field states* of awareness – each which their own unique mood or 'feeling tone'. All localised somatic symptoms or emotional feelings give expression to such field states of awareness - which we can sense and resonate with through a type of somatic *field resonance* that has the nature of what Sheldrake calls 'morphic resonance' – being a resonance of outer form (*morphe*) on the one hand and inner mood or feeling tone on the other.

When we see someone hunched up or laid back, smiling or frowning, laughing or crying, rigid or relaxed, then their posture and facial expression not only gives outer *form* to an inner tone of feeling, this tends induces a *similar feeling tone* in us through somatic field resonance, understood as 'morphic resonance' - a resonance of outward form (*morphe*) and inner feeling tone. The induction of a particular feeling tone in us through sensitivity to the expressive bodily form or 'language' of another may in turn find expression in us mirroring some aspect of their body language. Thus a smile tends to make us smile, weeping to make us weep, a tense or relaxed muscular posture to make us tense up or feel more relaxed, a shrill voice or rapid speech to make up speak in a shriller tone or more rapid way. The art of *consciously* mimicking and/or mirroring a person's facial expression and body language - down to its finest and subtlest details – the merest gleam of a particular look in someone's eyes for example - that enables us, within and within our own bodies, to directly *sense and resonate* with what these body signs show. What they show is a particular tone and texture of the other person's own body self-awareness – not just their way of comporting themselves bodily but their way of feeling themselves bodily.

From a soma-semiotic perspective it cannot be sufficiently emphasised that every bodily state – not least when a person is ill – is at the same time a both *state of consciousness* and a 'self state' – a way of feeling themselves – and vice versa. Every mental or psychological state and every state of conscious – even a state of seeming detachment or dissociation from the body – is at the same time a bodily or somatic state, one that can be sensed in a bodily way.

The Resonant Healing Process

Soma-semiotics understands the human organism as the instrument or *organon* with which we give shape and form to qualities and tonalities of awareness – whether in the form of words, dreams and mental images, bodily gestures or somatic symptoms. Therapy is understood as an *organismic healing process* leading from *soma-sensitivity* to the words and body language of the patient to *somatic resonance* with their own inwardly sensed body and self. Somatic resonance in turn is what facilitates a *transformative response* on the part of the therapist. What I call 'organismic healing' therefore is a 'resonant healing process' or process 'transformative resonance' that proceeds in three stages.

1. **Soma-sensitivity**
2. **Somatic resonance**
3. **Transformative response**

These stages require a trained and cultivate capacity on the part of the therapist to (a) *sense and resonate* with the patient's felt bodily sense of dis-ease, (b) *transform* their own bodily sense of self from one of dis-ease to one of ease, and (c) use somatic *field resonance* to intentionally effect a felt transformation in the patient's own bodily sense of self.

The therapist may, for example, may find themselves outwardly sensing and then inwardly resonating with a quality of frozen immobility in the sensed body of the patient. Only by first sensing and coming to *resonate* with this sense of 'frozen immobility' – feeling it within and within in their *own* felt body – can the therapist then begin to *gradually and intentionally* transform their own bodily sense of self from one of 'frozen immobility' to one of 'warm fluidity' or 'fluid warmth' – and gradually *impart* this fluid 'warmth of feeling' to the patient through the resonant 'bi-personal field' established through the initial state of resonance. The key word here is 'gradually'. For it is only through establishing and *staying* in resonance with the patient's felt dis-ease that the practitioner can (a) begin to evoke within themselves and impart to the patient a new bodily sense of self to the patient, and (b) see and sense the degree to which their own transformative response is indeed exerting such a healing effect through resonance. If this is not the case, then the therapist must start from the beginning again – going through the three states of soma-sensitivity, establishing somatic resonance, and then seeking again to evoke and impart a new and transformed sense of self to the client through the bi-personal field.

Central to the art of transformative resonation is therefore the therapist's awareness of the dyadic or bi-personal field of awareness between their own body and that of the patient. If the therapist is successful in sensing and resonating with the patient's felt dis-ease this resonance will be experienced by both patient and practitioner as *a shift* in the felt quality of the dyadic field. For the therapist's successful somatic *resonance* with a particular quality of the patient's felt dis-ease will automatically *amplify* their own and the patient's own awareness of it – not least if the therapist has learned to precisely *mirror* the patient's dis-ease through their face and eyes. For if the therapist is themselves able to give precise and resonant giving bodily expression to the patient's disease, then both therapist and patient will find themselves in deeper resonance with it – and with each other. This is where the therapist's range and mobility of body language – in particular the language of the face and eyes – is so important.

The Separation of Psychotherapy and Somatic Medicine

In what relation do psychotherapists and 'mental health' professionals stand to the biomedical model of illness, and in particular to the medical treatment of somatic symptoms? The question is a politically charged one, because the professional boundary between somatic medicine and psychotherapy is one closely guarded by the medical establishment. Many mental health professionals still defer to medical authority and the medical model, at least when it comes to so-called physical illness. This is something of a paradox given that:

1. on the one hand large number of patients present with symptoms seen as 'psychosomatic' by their doctors themselves.

2. one the other hand, most physicians completely *lack* the 'soma-sensitivity' necessary to sense and resonate with the patient's felt dis-ease (e.g. the felt 'loss of heart' that may be expressed and embodied through overt 'signs' of physical heart disease)/

Psychotherapists and counsellors of course, tend precisely *not* to be sought out by patients who see their symptoms as purely somatic, and their 'illness' as something purely 'physical'. Many people recognise that the institutionalised division between psychotherapy and somatic medicine, mental and physical illness, is an artificial one. Until now however, there has existed no framework of thought that truly transcends the artificial separation of 'mind' and 'body', 'psyche' and 'soma' – not only in theory but in therapeutic practice. Soma-semiotics provides such a framework, acknowledging as it does that the 'soul' or 'psyche' has its own independent bodily nature and exists as an independent body in its own right – the *psychical organism* or *psyche-soma*. The theoretical framework of soma-semiotics therefore provides keys to a fundamentally new understanding of 'psychosomatics',

Similarly, the practice of soma-sensitivity and somatic resonance – offer powerful keys to a fundamentally new approach to both psychotherapy and somatic medicine, both 'psychosomatic' medicine and 'somatic psychotherapy'. These practices embody the new semiotics of felt sense and the sensed body implicit in the work and methods of Eugene Gendlin, but applied not just to psychotherapy but also to medicine and to the *bodily relationship* of therapist and client, doctor and patient.

Appendix

....subjective biology and biosemiotics

Introduction

"The essence of biology can never be grounded
in biology as a science."

Martin Heidegger

It is *not* the purpose of this essay to explore in depth what
Heidegger sought to say through these words, which are
connected with his thinking regarding the relation between
science (and specific sciences) on the one hand, and philosophy
or thinking as such on the other. Instead my purpose is to look
at the social-historical and cultural context in which Heidegger's
own thinking evolved. For in the early part of the 20th century
the question of what constitutes 'biology as a science', indeed
what 'science' as such is, was a highly *controversial* one - not just

scientifically, but also philosophically, culturally and politically (not least in the context of Nazism). At the heart of the controversy surrounding biology as a science was the opposition between 'mechanistic' theories on the one hand and 'vitalistic' theories on the other, together with the search for a *holistic* understanding of living organisms. This was something that Heidegger himself took a deep interest in, specifically naming two biologists, Hans Driesch and Jakob von Uexküll (1864-1944) whom he hailed as having accomplished, respectively: 'two decisive steps'.

"The first step concerns the recognition of the holistic character of the organism ... The second step is the insight into the essential significance of research concerned with how the animal is bound to its environment."

In relation to the second step – the work of Uexküll, Heidegger goes on to remark that:

"His investigations are very highly valued today, but they have not yet acquired the fundamental significance they could have if a more radical interpretation of the organism were developed on their basis."

He also adds that:

"It would be foolish if we attempted to impute or ascribe philosophical inadequacy to Uexküll's interpretations, instead of recognising that the engagement with concrete investigations like this is one of the most fruitful things that philosophy can learn from contemporary biology."

What "investigations" and 'interpretations" on the part of Uexküll is Heidegger referring to here, what "fundamental significance" belongs to them "if a more radical interpretation of the organism were developed on their basis", and in what did they perhaps allow Heidegger himself to "learn from contemporary biology"? These are important questions, not only because Uexküll's biology was in itself a most "radical interpretation of the organism" but also may have been the very inspiration and foundation of Heidegger's own most central philosophical notion: 'Being in the World'.

Uexküll's 'Decisive Step'

Harrington quotes an unpublished biographical note in which, looking at a beech tree during a walk through the Heidelberg woods, Uexküll suddenly had the thought that:

"This is not a beech tree but rather my beach tree, something that I, with my sensations, have constructed in all its details. Everything I see, hear, smell or feel are not qualities that exclusively belong to the beech, but rather are characteristics of my sense organs that I project outside of myself."

Whereas Darwinism saw evolution as a process by which organisms 'adapted' themselves to the environment, implying that organism and environment were distinct entities, Uexküll's 'decisive step' lay in showing that each species of organism dwells in its own *unique* 'surrounding world' or *Umwelt* – translated in English as 'environment'. This unique world is not merely an ecological 'niche' within 'the' environment. Rather it is a *world-in-itself*, a unique *subjective* world shaped by each organism's species-specific mode of sensory perception. Thus for a tick, for example, there is and can be no such thing in *its* environment as a rabbit, rat, cow, sheep or human being. Instead there is simply the smell of mammalian sweat, the tactile sense of mammalian hair and the sense of mammalian skin warmth. Thus for us the word 'mammal' is a mere generic *concept* – referring to a genus of sub-species such as rats and sheep, each of which we perceive as separate and distinct life forms in *our* humanly perceived environment. For a tick, on the other hand, 'mammalness' is an immediate sensory *percept*, one that is not differentiated into differently perceived sub-species.

As Uexküll himself put it, for human beings *"a mammal as a directly perceived object does not exist as such; mammal [for humans] is only an abstraction of thought, a concept that we use as a means of categorisation, but we could never encounter in life."*

It is in this way that Uexküll came to a more general question:

"Standing before a meadow covered with flowers, full of buzzing bees, darting dragonflies, grasshoppers jumping over blades of grass, mice scurrying and snails crawling about, we would instinctively tend to ask ourselves the question: Does the meadow present the same prospect to the eyes of all those different creatures as it does to ours?"

On a more general level then, what we humans perceive as 'the' environment through our own species-specific sense organs is simply not the same environment as perceived by other species. And our perception of other species within that environment is wholly different from *that of those other species themselves*. What we perceive and conceive as 'a shark'- in contrast to other oceanic life forms - bears no relation to the way a shark itself, with its capacity for electrical sensing or 'electroception', perceives the shape and form of other *sharks* - or that of any other oceanic life forms. The 'environing world' or 'environment' as subjectively perceived through the eye of a *fly* is in no way comparable in form and nature - either *spatially* or *temporally* – to the world as perceived by the human eye. Uexküll used the image of a 'soap bubble' as a metaphor for the unique 'environing world' or Umwelt perceived by each species of organism.

"Each of us carries this soap bubble around with himself his whole life long, like a sturdy shell. It is tied to us, as we to it. Within our soap bubbles, our suns rise and set for each of us. These suns are very variable."

Since *each* organism dwells in its own unique environing world or 'environment' *no* organism can in any way be thought of as separate from *its* perceptual environment. Thus for human beings to speak of 'the' environment' is to privilege our own specifically *human* mode of perception *over that of all other species* - despite the fact that many of these other species have organs of perception far more differentiated than or quite *different* to our own. For just as we have no capacity to perceive the electrical environment of a shark, the sonar environment of a bat or the vibrational environment of a snake, so we also have no way of perceiving the visual environment of a fly or the 'scent environment' of a dog – its sense of smell being so much more differentiated than our own.

Uexküll's decisive understanding of the organism's being as inseparable from its environing world makes one wonder to what extent his 'Umwelt' biology was itself decisive for Heidegger in coming to his own concept of being as 'being in the world'. For as Anne Harrington comments:

"Although the fact has not been widely recognised, the 1985 published version of Heidegger's 1929-1930 lectures shows that he had studied and digested Uexküll's works at remarkable length, particularly Theoretical Biology and Outer World and Inner World of Animals. It may well be, therefore, that Uexküll's concept contributed, in a way not yet properly recognised, to Heidegger's intriguingly similar concept of "Being-in-the-world", which Heidegger had first comprehensively articulated in Being and Time, published just a few years before the Freiburg lectures. Indeed, in a 1937 article, Uexküll would himself call attention to the similarities between his views and those of Heidegger. The timing of this belated recognition of affinities does not belie its truth but does suggest that Uexküll's motivation here was not purely that of intellectual generosity."

Taking Uexküll One Step Further

The radical *philosophical* implications of Uexküll's biology did not pass him by, constituting as they did a type of 'Copernican Revolution'.

"...I am afraid that if I publicly proclaim this perspective, that they will treat me à la Galileo, and either lock me up in a madhouse or else ridicule me as an arch-reactionary. However, I must just once say my piece. Perhaps no one will understand me anyway. Nevertheless, it remains a fact: 'Epur non si move.' I do not move around the sun, but rather the sun rises and sets in my arch of sky. The same thing occurs in a hundred thousand other such arches of sky."

And he clearly shares with Heidegger a distrust of all abstract mathematical notions of *space* divorced from the spatial field or horizon – the 'soap bubble' of our concrete subjective experiencing.

"Whether ... all of the ... claims that Einstein makes about a conceptual space without centre or coordination [are true], I am not in a position to verify – they do not interest me at all either, since this space, the more it distances itself from concrete [subjectively experienced] space, the more it forfeits its claims on reality."

Unlike Heidegger, on the other hand, he remained attached to the notion that the organism's sense organs 'project' a picture of its environing world outside themselves, rather than perception being, as Heidegger saw it, a matter of being directly immediately *there* where things themselves *are*.

"Everything I see, hear, smell or feel are not qualities that exclusively belong to the beech, but rather are characteristics of my sense organs that I project outside of myself."

This brings us to a *critical epistemological paradox* still ignored in *all* neurophysiological accounts of perception. For whilst these *begin* by assuming a world of pre-given objects 'out there' in physical space which our sense organs merely register and perceive, such theories then totally cut the ground from under their own feet by being forced to acknowledge that this pre-given world of objects – the supposed *source* of all sense data - is in fact nothing but a world picture projected outwards by the brain, and that all the things in it are nothing but phantasms of the brain. The paradox is clear. How can the sense organs register sense data from objects in the first place if those objects are, in the last analysis, and according to neurophysiological theory itself, nothing but projections of the brain?

Uexküll himself does not seem to acknowledge the inherent problem of the 'sense projection' model when he writes that:

"The eye...throws the picture that is produced on its retina out of itself into the visual space [surrounding] the animal. Sounds, smells, tastes and touch are all transposed out of the body and into the subjective space of the animal, proving in this way the existence of non-physical, that is to say, soul-like factors."

On the other hand however, it seems from the same citation that he has a clear inkling of a solution to this problem. This is indicated by his referring to the space in which the sounds, smells etc. are transposed as *"the subjective space of the animal."* For by taking as its very starting point the recognition that space is in itself essentially subjective – nothing more or less than a *spatial field* of awareness or subjectivity itself - and by recognising the primacy of different sensory spaces or fields of awareness - visual, auditory, olfactory etc. – subjective biology has no need to reduce them to a product or projection of localised 'sense organs', and nor does it need to posit any process of projection or transposition of sensory images 'out of the body' and 'into' subjective space. On the contrary it recognises sense organs such as the eye itself as perceptual phenomenon in themselves - manifesting from and within a visual space or field of awareness, and in this sense no different in principle from any other phenomena appearing within this field.

This brings us to a further paradox that remains unacknowledged and unaddressed in neurophysiological accounts of perception. This is the paradox that what science claims to know about the functioning of our sense organs and brain is itself derived from an external *perception* of those sense organs. What we know of or about the human eye for example, is shaped by the very way we perceive it *through* the human eye. Our knowledge of perceptual processes is therefore not only intrinsically circular but also necessarily shaped by our species-specific mode of perception – not only of the world but of the very *sense organs* with which we are supposed to perceive it.

What 'scientific' anatomy and physiology thus continues to blindly ignore is the simple reality that what we *perceive* as having the anatomical form and function of an eye or sense organ of any type - just as what we *perceive* of as having the form of a brain, nerve, cell or internal organ of any sort - is itself a product of our own species-specific *mode* of sense perception. The simple but unasked question implicit in this paradox is therefore this: if, as Uexküll recognised, what we perceive as a 'beech tree' - not our capacity to recognise it 'as' a beech tree but its actually perceived form and features - is a product of our own species-specific mode of human perception, then surely the same can be said of the way in which we perceive the bodily form and features of human beings - including both the human brains and the very organs of sense (the human eye for example) with which we perceive?

Within this 'epistemological' question lies an even more fundamental 'ontological' one. The question is what exactly it *is* that constitutes 'a shark' or 'human being', an 'eye' or 'brain' in the first place – given that the very way we 'objectively' perceive both different life forms and their organs is, again, something shaped by our species-specific mode of perception? In answer to this question and from the perspective of a thoroughgoing *subjective biology* I believe we can take Uexküll's insights themselves a "decisive step" further. We can do so by recognising that what we perceive externally or 'exteroceptively' as anatomical forms of specific 'organisms' and their sense 'organs' are *in essence* not objective biological forms of 'living matter' but rather *organising field-patterns* of subjectivity or awareness as such. Every such organising *field-pattern of awareness* in turn shapes its own unique environing world or 'Umwelt' - understood as an organised or *patterned field of awareness.*

Uexküll had compared the environing worlds inhabited by different species and their members to 'soap bubbles'. The example of human perception of a beech tree (*"This is not a beech tree but rather my beech tree"*) could be taken as implying a type of solipsism of individual subjective worlds or soap bubbles - one which denies reality to the beech tree as such, or treats it, in Kantian fashion, as an unknowable 'thing in itself'. This objection can be overcome through the recognition that what each life form perceives as the same or another life form in the 'soap bubble' of its environing world can be understood simply as its own way of *giving* perceptual form – through its own *patterned field of awareness* – to the specific *field-pattern of awareness* that essentially *is* that other life form, whether a member of its own species or not.

Diagram 1 illustrates the way in which individual members of species perceive one another within the respective 'soap bubbles' of their environing world. The two larger circles represent the environing worlds or 'field patterns of awareness' of two life forms, similar or different. The smaller circles within the larger ones represent how, in a manner shaped by the *patterned field of awareness* that *is* the 'soap bubble' of its environing world, each life form perceives or gives a specific perceptual form to the specific organising *field-pattern of awareness* that each and every life-form (indeed every perceived phenomenon) essentially *is*. The diagram, in other words, shows in principle the dialectical *interrelation* between the environing or 'soap bubbles' of two or more life forms – the perceptual *form* that each takes *within* the environing world of the other.

Diagram 1

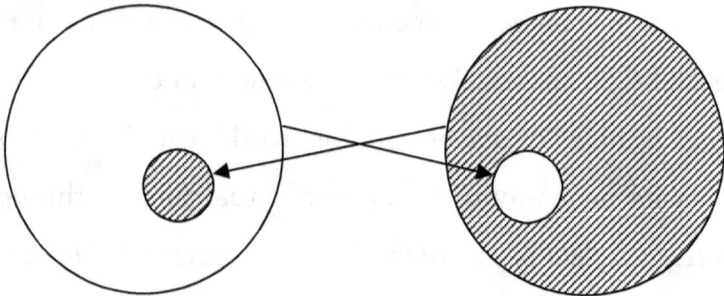

The Ocean of Awareness

A big question remains to be answered however. This is the question of what constitutes the *surrounding medium* – that *within which* the seemingly separate 'soap bubbles' or environing worlds of different life forms exist. Here we can call upon the analogy – actually no *mere* analogy - of an *ocean*. Every fish or oceanic life form perceives not only other life forms but also the *ocean itself* in its own way – a way shaped by its own *defining field-pattern of awareness.* What then constitutes the ocean *as such* - in contrast to the way it is perceived or experienced by the different life-forms within it? Subjective biology argues that the ocean as such is essentially nothing more or less than a larger *field of awareness* from and within which every life form – understood as a specific field-pattern of awareness – takes shape. As an *ocean of awareness,* the *ocean as such* is a field of countless *potential* field-patterns of awareness, each and all of which then take on for one another – and in very different ways – the actual perceptual shape or patterning of a specific oceanic life-form or phenomenon.

Subjective biology then, is not a reduction of different life-forms to *separable* 'subjects', each inhabiting their own *separate* subjective world. For just as the ocean is the source of all the life-forms that inhabit it, so also, understood as an ocean of awareness, is it the source of all the perceptual field patterns and patterned fields of awareness that define these life forms. Each life form is *not just* related to all others through the way in which they 'externally' manifest to one another within the soap bubbles of their own unique perceptual worlds. They are also 'inwardly' related to one another by virtue of sharing an inner relation to the larger oceanic field of awareness *that is their common source.*

They can only give perceptual form (*morphe*) to one another only by virtue of *resonance* with each other as those *potential* patterns of awareness which *constitute* this common source – for these potential patterns of awareness are neither separable entities or subjects and yet nor are they merged into some indistinct or undifferentiated unity. Instead they are both *distinct* and *inseparable* – defined and thereby also intrinsically related through their very *difference* from one another. And being parts of the same ocean of awareness that is their common source, they are also in this sense parts of one another. This is one way of understanding the following remark of Uexküll regarding the nature of what he, like Goethe, saw as a type or musical harmony or resonance uniting the underlying patterns of each type of organism in a singular orchestra of life:

"If the flower were not beelike and the bee were not flowerlike, the harmony between them could never be achieved."

Subjective Biology and 'Morphic Resonance'

Uexküll himself referred to basic patterns of life that he called 'blueprints' (*Baupläne*). Similarly, the contemporary biologist Rupert Sheldrake speaks of them as 'morphic' or 'morphogenetic fields' and has coined the term 'morphic resonance' to describe the new principle of life they offer us insight into. My understanding of this principle is that the perceived biological form (*morphe*) of any organism is stabilised by *resonance* with those invisible 'blueprints' or patterns of the sort that Sheldrake calls 'morphic fields'. The difference between subjective biology and the biology of both Uexküll and Sheldrake is that I understand these *formative* fields, patterns or 'blueprints' subjectively, i.e., not as hypothetical forces incapable of experimental measurement and inaccessible to direct awareness - but rather as organising field patterns and patterned fields *of awareness as such*. Everything from supposedly 'insentient' atoms and molecules to single cells and multi-cellular organism - is understood in subjective biology as the expression of field patterns and field qualities of atomic, molecular, cellular and organic *awareness*. This awareness however is pre-reflective and pre-egoic - it is not the property of atomic, molecular or cellular egos or subjects. And yet it is an awareness tuned and toned in a specific way, defined by a specific tonality or feeling tone. That is why Uexküll himself spoke of cells and organisms, not as possessing a human-type ego or 'I' but rather a unique *Ich-ton* or 'I-tone'.

Morphic Resonance and Musical Medicine

The *organising field patterns of awareness* that constitute the essence of any *organism* (a word that has its root in the Greek *organon* – a musical instrument) can in this sense be likened to organising *musical patterns* of tones, each with their own specific *tonal qualities*. Vocal or music tones have felt tonal *qualities* of warmth or coolness, hardness or softness, heaviness or lightness, darkness or brightness, flatness or sharpness, angularity or roundness, dullness or clarity, and mutual harmony and disharmony - *resonance or dissonance*. Subjective biology understands the experience of dis-ease *musically* – as a sensing of patterns and qualities of *feeling tone*. It is tonalities of cellular and organic *awareness* - and their sensed and sensual *qualities* such as warmth and coolness of feeling, brightness and darkness of feeling etc. – that then find expression as specific *sensations* such as heat or coldness, light and darkness. Similarly, it is the organism's immediate senses of muddied, dissonant, disharmonious or disordered 'patterns' of feeling tone that find expression as medical 'disorders', whether 'mental' or 'physical'. This is because felt tonal qualities and patterns of cellular *awareness* find expression not only in recognisable qualities and patterns of voice tone, but also in cellular and muscular 'tonus' or skin and organ 'tone'. Of course, sensed qualities of vocal tone are *themselves* an expression of the muscular *tonus* of the vocal organs of the organism as a whole, which is why we sense and speak of someone 'sounding' well or unwell – or, seeing the pallor of their skin or sensing a lack of tonus in their muscles and posture, sense and speak of them as 'looking' unwell. What Sheldrake calls 'morphic resonance' therefore, can be understood in its essence as a relation of resonance or dissonance between *form* and *feeling tone* - understanding 'feeling tone' as felt tonal qualities and patterns of organismic *awareness*. The enormous and still untapped healing power of *music* lies in the way it can give resonant form or expression to states of dis-ease – for example to dissonant, dull or 'painfully' sharp tones of feeling awareness – and in this way *remove* the need for their expression in organic, bodily sensations and disorders.

Heidegger and 'Biosemiotics'

The term 'biosemiotic' derives from the Greek *bios* (life) and *semeion* (mark or sign). It was first coined by F.S. Rothschild, who proposed that subjective experiencing, far from being an inexplicable *product or property* of observable neurological activity. structures, functions and processes was but a living biological *sign or symbol* of those processes. Today 'biosemiotics' is a generic term for a multiplicity of theories and models all of which emphasise the communicative or sign character of all biological processes and interactions, both in contrast to - or in a way often confused with – molecular and genetic reductionism. For although they may makes use of linguistic or 'semiotic' terms such as 'expression', 'marker', 'signalling', 'message', 'messenger', 'recognition' etc. many such theories use them as mere *metaphors* for wholly non-subjective and purely mechanistic-cybernetic processes of molecular 'information' exchange, regarding them - in contrast to soma-semiotics - as biological 'sign' processes devoid of any dimension of subjectively sensed meaning or 'sense'.

The German word 'Sinn', like the English word 'sense', has a double sense. On the one hand it serves as a synonym for meaning. On the other hand it is used to speak of specific perceptual 'senses' and 'sense organs'. Uexküll was among the first to unite these two senses of the words 'Sinn' and 'sense', and that in a manner most closely akin to Heidegger. Heidegger himself speaks in the Zollikon Seminars of human existing or *Da-sein* as *"a capacity to receive-perceive the significance of the things that are given to it and that address it..."* [my stress] adding that as such *"it is not something which can be objectified at all under any circumstances."* And the reason that Uexküll is regarded today as the pioneer of what is termed 'biosemiotics' - the understanding of life as a language or sign system - is the fact that he did not *separate* the physiological functioning of the sense organs from the *significance* of whatever was sensed by the organism - but instead recognised the essentially 'semiotic' or *sign-character* of every sensory cue (*Merkmal*) that an organism was open to "receive-perceive".

Heidegger is also renowned for having emphasised the active and practical character of our "being-in-the-world" and of our relation to the things in it. Thus a hammer is not 'a hammer' by virtue simply of being some 'actual' object that is "present to hand" and just happens to be called 'a hammer'. Instead what makes a hammer 'a hammer' is that it is "ready to hand" – no mere *actually* present object but something that can *potentially* be grasped, picked up and practically *used* in the particular way that first defines it *as* a hammer. The *sign-character* of the hammer is no mere property of its perceptual form but has to do with the *practical significance* of that form as a tool or instrument for actively changing the environment of the user. As for Uexküll, the sign character of specific sensory cues or *Merkmale* for an organism lay in the way they were enacted through the activation of specific motor responses or *Wirkmale* – responses that in turn *altered* the environment of the organism, in this way also opening it to fresh sensory cues and also triggering new motor responses - thus resulting in a further "Functional Circle" of *Merkmale* and *Wirkmale*, of sensory cues or signs from the sensory environment and motor responses that in turn bring new sensory cues to the fore.

Thus a tick's initial olfactory sense of the smell of mammalian sweat has a sign character with immediate meaning or sense, a sense that is immediately *enacted* by dropping down onto the mammal. This brings the tick into tactile contact with the mammal's hair - thus foregrounding a different type of sensory sign or cue in its Umwelt. The sensed significance of this new tactile sign in is enacted by the way the hair guides the tick to the heat it senses from the mammal's skin – which in turn acts as a sensed sign for the tick to begin sucking its blood.

All this does not imply however, that the meaning or sense of sensory experiencing can be reduced to the *sign* character of what is perceived – to seeing something 'as' a hammer for example, irrespective of the particular shape, form and other sensory qualities of this *specific* hammer. This is a human prejudice. For a tick or any other species of life, the *sign* character of what is perceived is precisely that what is *sensed*.

The experiential world of the tick, in contrast to that of the human being, is a world of directly *sensed significance* and not of already *signified senses*. The tick does not recognise a mammal as 'a mammal' *in the same way* that a human being recognises a hammer as 'a hammer'. For us as human beings, the sign character of the hammer dominates its sensory features completely. Unlike the tick we can designate this sign character by naming the hammer as a hammer. We also recognise it as belonging to a whole generic class of 'tools' that form part of its worldly significance, as well as breaking down its component parts and materials, which for us also have a sign character – indicating the strength, durability, value or even commercial brand of the hammer.

The Medical Significance of the 'Functional Cycle'

From the world of the tick to that of human beings seems like a large step, and yet the clinical encounter of patient and physician reveals the same 'functional' or 'bio-semiotic' cycle' that Uexküll identified in the world of animals - yet with one significant difference. To begin with the human being becomes aware of something significant in its environing world (a particular life problem for example) that evokes a felt bodily sense of *dis-ease*. But then unlike the animal the human being selectively and consciously *assigns* a negative significance to something in its Umwelt, and/or *enacts* its bodily sense of dis-ease through *giving* it a *sign character* - that of a possible disease 'symptom'. Going to the doctor is the way in which the patient then *enacts* this already *signified sense* of their dis-ease symptoms. The patient's aim in going to the doctor is to either determine or seek confirmation of the *sign* character of their symptoms in a purely *biomedical sense* i.e., one which allows the physician to collude with the patient in reducing the felt meaning or sense of the patient's dis-ease to signs of a recognised disease.

This however, only completes and reinforces the three-stage *semiotic cycle* which defines the biomedical approach to illness i.e. (1) a patient *experiencing* a sense of dis-ease evoked within their life world as a whole (2) the patient *embodying* this sensed dis-ease in the form of a specific bodily symptom or *enacting* it through some form of symptomatic behaviour, and (3) *presenting* or *representing* the symptom to a physician as a potential diagnostic *sign* of some purely bodily and/or behavioural *disease* wholly *unconnected* with the patient's life world as a whole. In this way the medically *signified sense* that may be attached to a patient's symptoms is *superimposed* on the *life significance* of the dis-ease they express. These purely biomedically signified senses or meanings of the patient's life dis-ease are then *mutually enacted* though further stages in the *medicalisation* of the patient's life dis-ease, for example through multiple forms of medical testing and treatment – turning the human being's individual life world and dis-ease into a mere 'case' of a generic 'disease'. Here what I call the 'soma-semiotics of felt sense' – of directly *sensed significance* - runs up against a dominant biomedical and 'biosemiotic' model of meaning, one in which the sole object of interest is the sign character or already *signified sense* of sensory experiencing.

What is 'Life'?

In the German language the word for life (*Leben*) is part of a family of words which include *Leib* (translated as the 'lived body') and *Erleben* (to experience). The 'life-world' or *Lebenswelt* of the organism as *Leib* is first and foremost an *Erlebenswelt*, an 'experiential world', a world of subjective experiencing which is in no way bounded by its body as *perceived from without* (something that is anyway determined by the modes of perception of the species perceiving it) but is ultimately identical with its entire *Umwelt* or 'environing world'. Conversely, the organism as *Leib* or lived body itself is not only the body as *subjectively* experienced but also and essentially an *experiencing* body. Life, as vitality - as liveliness or *Lebendigkeit* – is essentially a liveliness and intensity of experiencing or *Erleben* as such, one which makes no distinction between pleasure and pain. Life recognises no opposition or duality between 'pleasure' and 'pain'. Illness – a tumour for example - is just as much an expression of the *life* of the organism as what is ordinarily defined as 'health' or as a healthy 'cell'.

The idea of *medicine* as something aimed principally at the *preservation* of 'life' is Darwinistic through and through, reflecting a basic concept of life itself as ruled, if not tautologically *defined*, by a principle of *self-preservation* – whether the self-preservation of an organism, species or a 'selfish gene'. Yet if the life (*Leben*) of the organism is something that is constantly and dynamically unfolding and transforming as a world of experiencing (*Er-leben*) it is no 'body', 'thing' or '*self*' in *need of preservation* in the first place. 'Life' as such is nothing that can be threatened destroyed – only the *form* that it takes at any given time. Yet such change of form or *trans-formation* is also something that belongs to the very essence *of* life itself. Life is the emergence, appearance or actualisation within awareness of new forms, shapes or patterns *of* awareness. Death is the disappearance or 'de-mergence' of old forms. Thus life and death too, are not opposites. And of course the entire 'world of nature' reveals nothing if not the vital place of *death* in natural *life*, just as without the constant death of cells, the life of the body itself would not be sustained.

The Subjective Symphony of Life

Uexküll dared take even these insights a decisive step further, arguing that the 'blueprints' of life – equivalent to Sheldrake's 'morphic fields' - survived the death of their manifest biological forms. That he formulated this belief with the words *"the immortality of the soul ... is absolutely certain"* indicated also an acknowledgement of the subjective or 'soul' character of these blueprints - something that subjective biology reinforces by understanding them precisely as organising field-patterns *of* awareness. And like Pythagoras and Goethe, Uexküll also recognised the *musical* character of any organism as an instrument or *organon* emerging from and orchestrated by a larger cosmic and worldly *symphony of life* - one which subjective biology understands not as a static 'score' or 'blueprint', but rather as an ever-unfolding and ever-transforming field of 'inner sounds' – these being what give shape and pattern to feeling tones. The human body too is not just capable of hearing and uttering sounds. Rather it is itself uttered and sounded into manifestation from a world of inner sounds – of tonal shapes and field patterns of awareness. Thus the composer of a symphony or song does not simply produce music from his head and then merely write it down with his body to have it performed – sounded - by players and their instruments. Instead his entire bodily organism is itself and already an *embodiment* of 'the music of the soul' – giving individualised expression to that ever-unfolding and transforming symphony of awareness or subjectivity that *is life itself.*

'Subjective Biology' then, is a recognition of nature, life and the human organism as the expression of a living 'symphony' of subjectivity or soul itself, composed of inner sounds and feeling tones of a sort which resound in but can in no way be reduced to physical sounds or the signs of musical notation. This great subjective symphony of tones and chords of feeling awareness or soul does not have its source in either man or nature, mind or matter – but is instead the trans-physical *source* of both – a source both formative and transformative.

Bibliography

Anzieu, Didier *Psychic Envelopes* Karnac 1990

Aron and Anderson (ed.) *Relational Perspectives on the Body* The Analytic Press 1998

Boadella, David *Lifestreams* Routledge 1987

Buber, Martin *I and Thou* T&T Clark 1996

Buber, Martin *Between Man and Man* Routledge Classics 2002

Buber, Martin *Eclipse of God* Humanities Press International 1988

Buber, Martin *On Intersubjectivity and Cultural Creativity* University of Chicago 1992

Boss, Medard *Existential Foundations of Medicine and Psychology* J. Aronson

Breggin, Peter *Toxic Psychiatry* HarperCollins 1993

Buckman and Sabbach, *Magic or Medicine* Pan Books 1994

Campbell & McMahon *Bio-Spirituality* Loyola Press 1997

Chiozza, Luis *Hidden Affects in Somatic Disorders* Psychosocial Press 1998

Chiozza, Luis *Why Do We Fall Ill – The Story Hiding in the Body* Psychosocial Press 1999

Crabtree, Adam *From Mesmer to Freud* Yale University 1993

Fiumara, G. C. *The Metaphoric Process – Connections between Language and Life* Routledge 1995

Dürckheim, Karlfried *Hara, The Vital Centre of Man* Allen and Unwin 1980

Foucault, Michel *The Birth of the Clinic* Routledge 1989

Cooper, Robin (Ed.) *Thresholds between Philosophy and Psychoanalysis* Free Association Books 1989

Gadamer, Hans-Georg *The Enigma of Health* Stanford University Press 1992

Garfinkel, Harold *Studies in Ethnomethodology* Prentice-Hall 1967

Gendlin, Eugene *Focusing* Bantam 1979

Gendlin, Eugene *Experiencing and the Creation of Meaning* Northwestern University Press 1997

Gordon, Paul *Face to Face; Therapy as Ethics* Constable and Company Ltd. 1999

Goldstein, Kurt *The Organism* with foreword by Oliver Sacks, Zone Books 1995

Harrington, Anne *Reenchanted Science – Holism in Germany from Wilhelm II to Hitler* Princeton 1996

Heidegger, Martin *Zollikoner Seminare* Klostermann 1994

Heidegger, Martin *Zollikon Seminars* transl. Mayr and Askay Northwestern University Press 2001

Heidegger, Martin *The Fundamental Concepts of Metaphysics* Indiana 1995

Heidegger, Martin *The Principle of Reason* Indiana University Press 1996

Heidegger, Martin *The Question Concerning Technology* trans. Lovitt Harper Torchbooks 1977

Heidegger, Martin *Contributions to Philosophy* trans. Emad and Maly, Indiana University Press 1999

Heron, John *The Phenomenology of Social Encounter: the Gaze* Philosophy & Phenomenological Research. Vol. XXXI, No. 2, December, 1970

Hoffmeyer, Jesper *Signs of Meaning in the Universe* Indiana 1993

Husserl, Edmund *The Crisis of the European Sciences and Transcendental Phenomenology* Northwestern University Press 1970

Illich, Ivan *Limits to Medicine: Medical Nemesis – The Expropriation of Health* Marion Boyars 1995

Kay, Lily *Who Wrote the Book of Life?* Stanford University Press 2000

Kosok, Michael *Dialectics of Nature* Proceeding of the Telos Conference 1970

Kuriyama, S. *The Expressiveness of the Body and the Divergence of Greek and Chinese Medicine* Zone Books 2002

Lakoff and Johnson *Metaphors We Live By* University of Chicago Press 1980

Lewontin, R.C. *Biology as Ideology, the doctrine of DNA* Harper 1993

Levin, David Michael *The Body's Recollection of Being* Routledge 1985

Lowen, Alexander *Bioenergetics* Penguin Books 1994

Maslow, Abraham *Toward a Psychology of Being,* 3rd Ed., John Wiley and Sons, 1999

Mindell, Arnold *Working with the Dreaming Body* Arkana 1989

Reich, Wilhelm *The Function of the Orgasm* Souvenir Press 1983

Roberts, Jane *The Nature of Personal Reality* Amber-Allen 1994

Roberts, Jane *The Way Toward Health* Amber-Allen 1997

Roberts, Janine *Fear of the Invisible* 2008

Shapiro, Kenneth J. *Bodily Reflective Modes* Duke University Press 1985

Sheldrake, Rupert *A New Science of Life - The Hypothesis of Morphic Resonance* Park Street Press 1995

Svenaeus, F. *The Hermeneutics of Medicine and the Phenomenology of Health: Steps Towards a Philosophy of Medical Practice,* Kluwer Academic Publishers 2000

Tauber, Alfred *The Immune Self: theory or metaphor?* Cambridge 1997

Weizsäcker, Viktor *Warum wird man krank?* Suhrkamp 2008

Zigmond, David *Three Types of Encounter in the Healing Arts* Journal of Holistic Medicine, April/June 1987

Other books and articles by Peter Wilberg:

Heidegger, Medicine and 'Scientific Method'
New Gnosis Publications 2005

The Awareness Principle – a Radical New Philosophy of Life, Science and Religion New Yoga Publications 2008 / New Gnosis Publications 2009

The QUALIA Revolution – from Quantum Physics to Qualia Science Second Edition, New Gnosis Publications 2008

The Therapist as Listener – Heidegger and the Missing Dimension of Counselling and Psychotherapy Training New Gnosis Publications 2005

The New Yoga – Tantra Reborn – The Sensuality and Sexuality of our Immortal Soul Body New Yoga Publications 2009 / New Gnosis Publications 2009

The New Yoga of Awareness – Tantric Wisdom for Today's World New Yoga Publications / New Gnosis Publications 2009

Meditation and Mental Health – an introduction to Awareness Based Cognitive Therapy New Yoga Publications 2010/New Gnosis Publications 2010

The Science Delusion – Why God is Real and Science is Religious Myth New Gnosis Publications 2008

Event Horizon – Terror, Tantra and the Ultimate Metaphysics of Awareness New Yoga Publications 2008 / New Gnosis Publications (2008)

Heidegger, Phenomenology and Indian Thought
New Gnosis Publications 2008

Deep Socialism – A New Manifesto of Marxist Ethics and Economics New Gnosis Publications 2003

From New Age to New Gnosis – Towards a New Gnostic Spirituality New Gnosis Publications 2003

Head, Heart and Hara – the Soul Centres of West and East New Gnosis Publications, 2003

The Language of Listening Journal of the Society for Existential Analysis 3

Introduction to Maieutic Listening Journal of the Society for Existential Analysis 8.1

Listening as Bodywork Energy and Character; Journal of Biosynthesis 30/2

The Language of Listening Journal of the Society for Existential Analysis 3

Further on-line articles and resources:

www.existentialmedicine.org

www.thenewtherapy.org.uk

www.ingramcontent.com/pod-product-compliance
Lightning Source LLC
Chambersburg PA
CBHW070912270326
41927CB00011B/2535